"As followers of Christ, we must experience personal transformation before we can impact those around us. In *Counterfeit Comforts*, Robia Scott's refreshing transparency about her own journey and the inner struggles she faced as a professional dancer and actress provide specific, creative and very practical insights that will help anyone struggling with the process of change to get on the path toward healing and the recovery of their God-given identity and destiny!"

Ed Silvoso, president, Harvest Evangelism
and the International Transformation Network

"With candor, sensitivity and lessons learned from once being in the 'counterfeit pit,' Robia Scott boldly exposes the enemy's pitfalls and strategies that cause us to seek emotional comfort and validation in all the wrong places. The book is a practical and convicting beacon of hope."

Deborah Smith Pegues, bestselling author,
30 Days to Taming Your Tongue

"While reading this amazing book, I was struck by the incredible marriage of the depth and simplicity that would appeal to any person in any situation. There is a beauty of substance and style that Robia communicates to reach people where they are to get them to their God-given potential. Each chapter has riveting statements of life-changing principles that will be easily remembered. *Counterfeit Comforts* will launch you into the depth of joy and truth that is the real thing, better than any counterfeit!"

Dan Fessler, lead pastor, Waters Community,
Sewell, New Jersey

COUNTERFEIT Comforts

Freedom from the Imposters That Keep You from True Peace, Purpose and Passion

Robia Scott

Chosen

a division of Baker Publishing Group
Minneapolis, Minnesota

Published by Chosen Books
11400 Hampshire Avenue South
Bloomington, Minnesota 55438
www.chosenbooks.com

Chosen Books is a division of
Baker Publishing Group, Grand Rapids, Michigan

Printed in the United States of America

Library of Congress Control Number: 2016938474

ISBN 978-0-8007-9812-3

Cover design by Dual Identity

Author is represented by Steven R. Lawson

16 17 18 19 20 21 22   7 6 5 4 3 2 1

To my husband, James,
who was worth the wait.

And I will pray the Father,
and he shall give you another Comforter,
that he may abide with you for ever.

John 14:16 KJV

Contents

Acknowledgments

To my spiritual posse: Charles Felix and a handful of loyal, dynamic, powerhouse women who stood lovingly and prayed ferociously to birth this book and this ministry into existence. You are a true spiritual family.

To Gina Keliher and Gwen Parsell: You have been pillars through it all and are the definition of faithful friends. And a special thank-you to Gwen Parsell for the hours you poured into the manuscript. This book would not be what it is if it had not been for you. You are the best freditor (friend/editor) a girl could have.

To Ed Silvoso for always making yourself available and for your gracious support. Steven Lawson for your wisdom and counsel in navigating new waters. David Sluka for steering my path and generously opening doors.

To Kim Bangs, Jane Campbell, Carra Carr, Shaun Tabatt, Dan Pitts, Natasha Sperling, Carissa Maki and all those at Chosen Books for your dedication to excellence and for partnering with me to bring this longtime dream to fruition.

And special thanks to my truly fabulous editor, Julie Carobini. You gently held my first book baby in your arms and with skill, warmth and encouraging words, nurtured it to maturity.

Introduction

I was living the dream—or so it seemed.

At twelve years old, I saw the movie *Flashdance* and from that moment I knew exactly what I wanted to do for the rest of my life: become a professional dancer. Inspired by the film to look the part, à la Jennifer Beals, I immediately permed my hair, cut up my sweatshirts and decided that leg warmers were the perfect accessory for every outfit. (If you remember the '80s, you know what I am talking about.)

I also began taking jazz, ballet and tap classes after school. Within a few years I was offered a dance scholarship at the prestigious Dupree Dance Academy in Hollywood, California, and at age sixteen I landed my first professional job. I was hired as a dancer in singer Debbie Gibson's music video for the song "Shake Your Love." Later I was signed by Prince (yes, *that* Prince) to star as "Pearl" in all of his music videos for the album *Diamonds and Pearls*. That led to traveling the world as one of his backup dancers.

After my tour with Prince ended, I felt I had reached my peak of success as a dancer, so at 22 years old, I retired from dance. I transitioned into acting and pursued the craft with the same fervency with which I had studied dance. A year later I began appearing on several popular TV shows.

But something was not right. I had a successful career as a dancer under my belt, and the next one, as an actress, was taking off. I had fame, financial security and everything that was supposed to bring fulfillment, happiness and comfort, but I was definitely not comfortable. I was tormented. I was obsessed with my body image, somewhat the norm for every woman, but being a dancer and actress multiplied the torment exponentially. My thought life revolved around what I ate, how I looked and what I weighed. I had become anxious, worried, fearful, a chain smoker, and though I was making a great living, I was in debt due to excessive spending.

I was a girl who seemed to have it all, and to have it all together. Though I may have appeared confident and in control, I was being controlled by food, controlled by cigarettes, controlled by emotions, and, truthfully, I felt completely out of control. My deepest desire was to find freedom, to be at rest on the inside and feel at ease with myself and with my life.

For a time, I sought spirituality in the New Age movement prevalent in Southern California. I also read self-help books, but nothing I was doing or reading was helping me in the areas in which I found myself struggling. I finally had to be honest with myself and admit that my best thinking and figuring only dug me into a deeper hole. I realized then that, in order to help myself, I needed something or Someone bigger than I.

No problem can be solved by the same level of consciousness that created it.

Albert Einstein

I had always believed in God, but knew there must be more to Him than I was currently experiencing. I was open and looking for answers.

Sometime later, I found myself sitting in a casting office with other actresses waiting to audition for a commercial. One of the women walked across the room to the water fountain. She was African American with short hair, and I noticed the words I AM tattooed on the back of her neck. Coming from the New Age movement, I was familiar with the lingo of positive affirmations. They all begin with "I am." I am the light, I am love, etc. Out of curiosity I asked her if her tattoo was New Age. "Oh, no, no, no," she replied. "I AM is the God of the Bible; when God was asked His name He replied, 'I AM.'" She pulled a small Bible out of her purse to show me. Then she started talking about Jesus. Instantly the room grew silent and a palpable tension overrode the light and easy atmosphere. The woman next to me shifted in her seat. Two gals sitting across from me shot each other a look, then stood up and walked outside. Funny how you can talk about Buddha, Kabbala and even witchcraft, and no one has a problem with it, but as soon as someone says "Jesus," people start to squirm. I did not understand everything my new friend said, but she was animated as she spoke, and I liked her. I asked her if she happened to know of a cool church. She did.

I joined her at church that Sunday, and the next, and the one after that. What I was hearing about God started to make sense—not perfectly—but the dots indeed began to connect, and once I had a few more Sundays under my belt, I made the decision to accept Christ. I became a Christian.

Still, I was nervous about what becoming "born-again" would entail. Would I have to sell my belongings and become a missionary in Africa? Would God tone down my personality and morph me into a cookie-cutter born-again version of myself? Could I still wear cute shoes?

One day I came across a story that quelled my fears and put my heart at ease. It was about Michelangelo, the artist who painted the Sistine Chapel, and who also sculpted the statue of *David,* among many other great works of art. Before Michelangelo began to sculpt, he would stand in front of his "canvas," a large block of marble, and stare into it. Before even picking up his chisel, he could "see" the finished work inside of that marble. Instead of trying to create the masterpiece, he simply removed the excess marble that was keeping it from being what it already was.

> I saw the angel in the marble and carved until I set him free.
>
> Michelangelo

That story brought a shift and a release for me. I realized that God works this way, too, and that surrendering my life to Christ did not mean that He would take away my personality, everything I loved and what ultimately made me *me.* Like Michelangelo, God only chips away at the excess: the fears, the addictions, the wrong belief systems, and the mental and emotional torment that hinder us from being the masterpieces He created us to be!

So my journey of faith began. What I had not been able to figure out on my own, God began to reveal. And then, in one moment of prayer, the Lord spoke something to me that changed my life forever. . . .

1

The Only Way To Is Through

The best way out is always through.

Robert Frost

I do not remember a time in my life when food was not an issue. At seven years old I could tell you the exact number of calories in a peanut butter and jelly sandwich along with every other food that went into my mouth. Becoming a dancer as a teenager only exacerbated the problem. The competition was fierce, and there was an exaggerated emphasis on weight and physical appearance. One particular day, I was eating lunch with my best friend in between ballet classes. We started off with salads, but ended up devouring a couple of huge brownies. Afterward, we decided to throw up. I don't know if we had learned about this practice on TV or heard about other girls doing it, but from that point on bulimia became another tool I used to control my weight. I did not force myself to vomit every day, but if I overate, the option was always there for me.

Fifteen years later, and two years into my walk as a Christian, my struggle with food had become worse than ever. Bulimia had grabbed ahold of me, and what used to be an occasional outlet now controlled me. My thoughts were consumed with my weight—what I would or would not eat, and how my body looked. Most of my thoughts in a day were centered on food. I was mentally tormented and could not have been further from freedom. Unfortunately, I seemed to get a lot of "nice" advice in church: pray more, read the Bible more. I was praying! I was reading the Bible! Neither was helping.

I did not understand how all my prayer, studying the Word, and church attendance could affect every area in my life—except my tortuous relationship with food. How could this be? Once I became a Christian, wasn't all the bad stuff supposed to go away or at least start getting better? Some of my darkest days occurred after I became a Christian. It was not supposed to be this way.

The Bible says that all the promises of God are available to me and that I can live in total freedom, and that is exactly what I expected. If I was giving my life and everything I had to God, then I expected God to give everything He had to me. Remaining in bondage in even one area of my life was unacceptable.

"Okay, Lord," I cried out, "what is the problem? You need to show me what is going on here; I need answers. I cannot continue to live like this. How do I get free?"

Then God answered me. Did that mean I heard an audible voice? No, but all of a sudden I had a sense in my spirit, and a thought came to my mind that I had never considered before:

You have too many counterfeit comforters.

What does that mean, too many counterfeit comforters? I had never heard that phrase before. I pondered it, and the Holy Spirit began putting the pieces together for me. In the Bible, one of the names of the Holy Spirit is Comforter. The Lord showed me that whenever I felt rejected, sad or disappointed, I did not go to the Holy Spirit for comfort, but to Mrs. Fields' cookies or to my good friends Ben and Jerry. (Chocolate fudge brownie ice cream, in particular.) I had developed a habit of running to something—anything—but primarily to food for an emotional release or to numb out so I would not have to feel anything at all. Then I heard this:

You do not have a food issue. You have a feelings issue.

The Lord began to show me how my food issue did not have to do with food at all. I had been trying to deal with my emotions by controlling food with dieting, binging and purging. We all know that does not work, at least not for long. When eating is out of control, the food itself is not the problem. The problem is using food for what it was never intended. Food is meant to nourish the body and fuel us—not to stuff down emotions, release stress or numb us out so we cannot feel anything at all. Food was not created to be our dear friend, our confidant or our companion in a lonely world.

I did not realize it, but I was using food to comfort myself, to take the edge off and to escape. The overeating was merely a symptom and not the problem. The binging was a reaction to something else. Trying to control the eating meant I was not dealing with the root of the problem, which is why dieting did not change me. Willpower worked for a while, but I would fall into the same pattern again and again no matter how hard I resisted. Dieting worked for a time, but the results were never lasting, because it is not about controlling the eating. It is about realizing why the eating is out of control.

19

Pain is an indicator of a problem. However, the second we feel the slightest discomfort, our knee-jerk reaction is to do anything to relieve us of pain as quickly as possible. In our culture we are obsessed with alleviating a symptom. We are trained by society and advertising to seek a remedy for every ailment and do whatever it takes to ease the pain. We are coerced to believe that it is best not to deal with pain, but to make ourselves feel better at any cost. We have all become expert escape artists. Advertising feeds on convincing us that every product will give us the relief, the satisfaction and the deep fulfillment we are looking for. Just like physical pain indicates a problem in our bodies, emotional pain signals like a bell—ding, ding, ding—that something is going on inside of us. Our goal should not only be to eradicate the pain, but to locate the root of the problem. It is natural for us to want to stop pain, but self-medicating only achieves temporary results, and at some point, the pain will resurface. The way to lasting results is to identify the source and go to work on that.

Why is dealing with our feelings so uncomfortable? Could it be that we were never taught how to deal with our feelings, so therefore the process feels unnatural? We spend years in school learning mass amounts of information, but rarely are we instructed in school, or even at home, for that matter, how to process our feelings—so much math and so few life lessons! The church could step in to fill the gap, but unfortunately, even in most churches, we are not taught how to process our feelings.

As Christians we understand that the result of knowing God should bring us peace and joy. This understanding, however, can increase the pressure on us to appear joy filled, so much that often we fake it. Inside the church people appear to be "fine." We are met at the front door by plastered-on smiles and bombarded by a cacophony of "praise the Lords." Ask

someone how he or she is doing, and the conversation goes
something like this:

"How are you, sister?"

"I'm blessed, you?"

"Blessed, blessed, blessed."

"Well, praise the Lord!"

Yikes! We all have a truth meter inside of us; we know when
we're getting the real deal and when we are not. All of us desire
true joy, but most of us have no idea how to achieve it. Wholeness does not transpire automatically. Breezing through the
church doors does not magically transform us. There are no
shortcuts in this process, and there is no side stepping around
it. The only way *to* peace, joy and righteousness is *through* a
little junk, gunk and funk.

We prefer to avoid the *through* part because, otherwise, we
might feel pain; but there is just no going around feelings.
Metaphorically speaking, you cannot get airlifted over the trash
dump and placed down in the flower bed. The price of peace
and authentic joy is a willingness to go through and go deep.

2

Into the Deep

I must be a mermaid. I have no fear of
depths and a great fear of shallow living.

Anais Nin

I remember the very first time Scripture came alive to me while reading the Bible. It was in the book of Luke, chapter five. This passage reveals more than just a few fishing tips. The Holy Spirit was talking to me about my life.

So it was, as the multitude pressed about Him to hear the word of God, that He stood by the Lake of Gennesaret, and saw two boats standing by the lake; but the fishermen had gone from them and were washing their nets. Then He got into one of the boats, which was Simon's, and asked him to put out a little from the land. And He sat down and taught the multitudes from the boat. When He had stopped speaking, He said to Simon, "Launch out into the deep and let down your nets for a catch."

But Simon answered and said to Him, "Master, we have toiled all night and caught nothing; nevertheless at Your word I will let down the net." And when they had done this, they caught a great number of fish, and their net was breaking.

Luke 5:1–6

The men had fished all night and caught nothing, yet Jesus told Simon to go fishing again and to let down his nets for a catch. Jesus instructed them to put out a little from the land. Then He told them to "launch out into the deep," and that is where they would come upon a great catch. A little from the land is not deep sea fishing. These men were not in deep waters. I understood the metaphor. Jesus revealed to me that in order to get to the good stuff, I, too, had to launch out into the deep. Deep was where I would come upon a great catch. Deep was where the abundance lay. Deep was where I had to be willing to go to find the freedom I had been looking for. Jesus asked them to push away from the land. Again the Holy Spirit personalized this for me. Pushing away from the land meant pushing away from the solid ground, from the secure and safe place, and meeting Jesus in unknown and unfamiliar waters. There is safety in shallow water. Shallow water is comfortable water. We have our footing, and there is no risk involved. Like everything in life, greatness and excellence means pushing past the norm and delving into uncharted and unfamiliar territory where most refuse to go. Unfamiliar often equals uncomfortable, but uncomfortable is the breeding ground for change. The Holy Spirit was beckoning me to leave my comfort zone, take a risk and launch out into the deep.

It is reassuring to note that Jesus did not send the fishermen out alone. He directed them into the deep, but He was in the boat alongside them the entire time. The same is true for us as we embark upon our unknown. As we venture into the deep, we don't have to fear. We are not alone. He is with us.

When you go through deep waters, I will be with you.

Isaiah 43:2 NLT

So, why does everything inside of us resist change and long to settle contentedly on the shores of familiarity? The first step in breaking free from our comfort zone is to be honest with ourselves and admit that we are not all that comfortable. The idea of having to face and feel our pain may seem intimidating and like a bunch of work, but the truth is denial is a full-time job. Change is scary, but not changing is scarier.

The amount of energy it takes to stifle emotions far surpasses the effort it would take to deal with them and find healing. Living a life cut off from ourselves is exhausting. Attempting to act okay when we are not okay saps the life from us. It is far less taxing to learn and then do what it takes to be okay. You might have to face some of the ugly stuff, but trying to avoid pain is a painful way to live. We think by stuffing our feelings we remain in control, but those feelings end up controlling us. They find their way to the surface and manifest in a myriad of ways—torment, addiction and depression. We try to circumvent them, but as you will see below, repressed feelings have a way of revealing themselves in unhealthy ways. The feelings you are not dealing with are dealing with you.

Feelings Revealed

Our squelched feelings reveal themselves through behaviors I call *counterfeit comforts*. There are many, many possible counterfeit comforts. Here are but a few:

Overeating	Drugs
Binging and purging	Cigarettes
Alcohol	Cutting yourself

Relationships	Exercise
Sex	Constant busyness
Shopping	Playing video games
Shoplifting	
Television	Gambling
Work	Reading magazines

As we go through our day, life happens. We experience discomfort and disappointment, and emotions stir within us. Instead of embracing all that we are feeling, we often look for an avenue to escape being uncomfortable. We each have our own drug of choice, our "thing," and we run to whatever that may be: a cigarette, or an entire pack of cigarettes, a donut or half a dozen donuts.

The pain of not changing is greater than the pain it takes to change.

Just as feelings are not inherently bad, many counterfeit comforts are not necessarily bad either. Exercise is healthy unless we are doing it compulsively to mask a deeper issue. Obviously seeking comfort through shoplifting or taking illegal drugs is never beneficial, but what about magazines, television and shopping? There is nothing wrong with reading a magazine, watching a TV show or buying an outfit. How could something as seemingly innocent as a fashion magazine be a counterfeit comfort? Is it bad to read a magazine? No, but if you are reading magazines for hours to disconnect and divert yourself from your life, then you are using magazines to avoid dealing with something. It is like being depressed and watching nine hours of television to zone out. Zoning out on occasion is not a bad thing. There is nothing wrong with watching a little TV at the end of a long day, but it is important to recognize the motive behind the action. It is not so much what we are doing, but why.

The Why Behind the What

Ask yourself, "Why am I turning to this? Am I doing this right now to escape and shut down?" This is not about deeming certain behaviors as bad or good. It is about realizing how even the most neutral behavior can be abused and used as a tool for evading. Let's be real—no one goes out on a Friday night and has ten drinks in order to relax and have a good time. Likewise, when you are standing over the kitchen sink shoving Oreo cookies into your mouth as fast as you can, it is not because you like Oreos. And when you have shopping bags next to your bed full of outfits that you bought two weeks ago, that you do not need and have not even hung up in the closet yet, it is not because you like clothes.

We have not failed, and we are not bad Christians for going to the counterfeits. We are not weak believers with little faith. We are hurting people trying to cope with life on this planet. Our loving Father in heaven understands and He has a lot of grace for us. It is easy at this point to look at your own counterfeit comforts and begin to feel guilty, but that is not the grace that God offers.

God is not mad at us for turning to counterfeit comforts.

You can drown your sorrows in chocolate chip cookies for the rest of time, and God will still adore you. Ice cream is not the devil; eating some ice cream is fine. Even if you eat a gallon of ice cream, God is not mad at you. You can eat ice cream until you are sick to your stomach, and the Lord still loves you. The reason He does not want us to go to a counterfeit comfort is not because He is a strict God who wants to control us. It is because He does not want to see us being controlled. God is not in the hellfire and damnation business. He is in the business of setting us free. Our Lord is wooing us to Him not only for comfort, but for healing. We can go to the Healer or get a temporary fix with a counterfeit comfort.

Counterfeit: An imposter; a pretender; unreal. An imitation intended to be passed off fraudulently or deceptively as genuine.

That is exactly what happens when we go to the counterfeit. We get deceived. We think we are getting something real, some true satisfaction, but the fulfillment always comes up short. The imposter can never give us what we are searching for, and like fish seeking food, we get lured in by the bait and hooked. God is not judging us; He is saying, "Come to Me. Instead of medicating, let Me heal you. You can take the edge off for now, or I can heal you forever." He is offering a better way. We either choose our counterfeit comforts, or we choose to deal with the issues and allow God to heal us. Only He can touch that place in us and leave us with something lasting. An emotional hole cannot be filled with anything but God. Vodka will not fill it, McDonald's will not fill it and the mall will not fill it. When we are empty and starving for love and for comfort, having something, anything at all, feels good—even if that something is the wrong thing.

A satisfied soul loathes the honeycomb, but to a hungry soul every bitter thing is sweet.

Proverbs 27:7

When a soul (the mind, will and emotions) is content, there are no cravings. Scripture goes so far as to say that when the soul is truly satisfied from within, it not only has no desire for the sweetness of the honeycomb, but it actually loathes it. But a soul that is empty and hurting looks for anything to ease the pain and fill that place. Just as when we are physically hungry any food sounds good, likewise, when a soul is hungry it will look to anything to take the edge off and fill the void. The following passage of Scripture tells how Esau sells his birthright, and sums up the counterfeit comforter perfectly:

Now Jacob cooked a stew; and Esau came in from the field, and he was weary. And Esau said to Jacob, "Please feed me with that same red stew, for I am weary." Therefore his name was called Edom. But Jacob said, "Sell me your birthright as of this day." And Esau said, "Look, I am about to die; so what is this birthright to me?" Then Jacob said, "Swear to me as of this day." So he swore to him, and sold his birthright to Jacob. And Jacob gave Esau bread and stew of lentils; then he ate and drank, arose, and went his way. Thus Esau despised his birthright.

Genesis 25:29–34

Esau was hungry, and in desperation to meet that hunger, he sold his birthright. He forfeited his position in life for a bowl of soup. He took the bait of instantaneous gratification and only after his stomach was full did he realize what he had done and what it had cost him.

When we are hurting, we are irrational. When we are in pain we make rash and emotional choices. We will do anything for some peace and satisfaction, and rarely do we consider the long-term consequences. It is only after we fill ourselves that the guilt of what we have done floods in. Then shame and sadness follow so we turn again to the counterfeit to alleviate that pain, which only brings more guilt and shame, and the cycle perpetuates.

So we find ourselves in a similar place as Esau: our lives and dreams stolen by the counterfeit and the cycle that has enslaved us. We have exchanged our future and our peace for temporary relief and fleeting, counterfeit comfort. We hate ourselves for it, but we cannot seem to break free.

The Holy Spirit's Power in Overcoming

Though in ourselves we are unable to break the bondage, there is a way in God. As we learn to lean on Him—and stand back and take our hands off of our lives somewhat—the true

Comforter will meet our needs and fill our emptiness. The cycle will then begin to break and we will be able to live within the freedom we have known possible, but haven't until now known how to attain. Through Him we are able to step back onto the path that leads to our destiny. In Him, we can overcome.

Using shopping to avoid feelings does not work. Using television to avoid feelings does not work. Using food to avoid feelings does not work. Turning to God and dealing with feelings is what works.We have to feel and deal in order to heal.

It's not easy, but it's worth it. Excellence is not gleaned by taking the easy road. Anyone who achieves mastery in any given area does what most people are not willing to do. Tom Hanks said it best in the movie *A League of Their Own* when his female ball players were complaining that baseball was difficult and what they had to face was too much.

> It's supposed to be hard. If it wasn't hard, everyone would do it. The hard is what makes it great.
>
> Tom Hanks, as Jimmy Dugan

It takes tenacity and drive to push against the status quo to achieve greatness; it takes courage to do whatever it takes to be free. You cannot go part way with God and receive total freedom. Make a decision in your heart that you are going all the way with God. No matter what it takes, you are going all the way, because total freedom demands total commitment.

> There is no such thing as part freedom.
>
> Nelson Mandela

3

The Choice Point

I have set before you life and death, blessing
and cursing; therefore choose life.

Deuteronomy 30:19

When I sought the Lord about my challenging relationship with food, the first thing the Holy Spirit told me was, "You have too many *counterfeit comforters.*"

The second was, "You don't have a food issue. You have a *feelings* issue."

It was the third thing He spoke to me that really threw me. I had been asking the Lord to take away my desire to overeat and binge. I was fervently praying for Him to deliver me from all addictive behaviors and loose me from all counterfeit comforts. Then in my spirit I heard, *Your praying is not going to help you.*

What? Was this a little interference, or was God telling me that prayer did not work? How could prayer not help me?

31

I began to ponder my prayer life regarding this issue, and recognized that I had created a fantasy scenario of how I wanted God to handle things. In the morning, I would pray whole-heartedly—with some begging and pleading thrown in—for God to take away my food issues. God would hear my prayers and help me by removing my desire to overeat. And then, on top of that, if need be, the Holy Spirit would show up on the scene while I was eating, and would supernaturally knock the fork out of my hand when it was time for me to stop.

Back to reality. It was not that prayer could not help me, but in this instance, I was praying from the wrong mindset. As I pressed deeper for an understanding of why praying this way was ineffective, I began to receive the revelation that I could pray, and pray, and *pray*, but all my prayers were not going to make God come in and just fix me. The power of prayer would not eliminate my freedom to choose. It was as if I had been praying for God to control me, but the Lord, the Author of free will, was not going to go against His nature by overriding the principle of free will that He had established. God had not been telling me that prayer did not work, but that it was understanding *how* prayer worked that would bring the desired result. The Holy Spirit began to show me that my way of praying in the morn-ing was not a magic wand that would make all my temptations go away. He said, "What prayer does is make you sensitive to the *choice point*. What you do at the choice point is up to you."

The Lord shifted my perspective in order for me to recog-nize that my time in prayer would make me sensitive to the still, small voice that is the Holy Spirit. Prayer would tune me in to that little check in my spirit from Him, the one gently nudging me to put down the fork and stop eating. This was my choice point: the Holy Spirit giving me the opportunity to make a different decision right at the moment when changing direction was still possible. This is what it means to walk in the

Spirit or to live a life tuned in to the Holy Spirit so we hear His voice and follow His lead. This is how we move outside of the realm of trying in our own strength—trying to change, trying to do the right thing. All my trying to fix myself through self-help, trying to stop binging and purging, and trying to quit chain smoking were to no avail. I needed God and the Holy Spirit to speak to me personally and show me the way out of the mess I had found myself in. It was much easier, and much more effective, to listen to God and be led by Him than to try and try and *try* in my own strength. Soon Scriptures like the one below began to make sense:

Walk in the Spirit, and you shall not fulfill the lust of the flesh.

Galatians 5:16

This verse in Galatians can be easily misinterpreted and cause much fear and pressure. This Scripture does not mean, "Get it right and stop being so fleshly or else, you bad, bad Christian!" This is not instruction from a mean God warning us to get it together, but from a loving Father teaching us how to overcome. Striving in the flesh is not the way to combat the flesh. You cannot fight the flesh with the flesh. You fight the flesh by walking in the Spirit.

If we live in the Spirit, let us also walk in the Spirit.

Galatians 5:25

I was praying that God would take away my desire to overeat. I was asking Him to make everything go away, to stop me from certain behaviors, and to make it so that I never felt tempted to binge again. And God can do that. There are times when He moves supernaturally upon us and in an instant we are transformed. Where in one touch of His garment we are made well (see Matthew 9:21).

But what I have found to be true is, in many instances, healing, especially in regards to emotional healing, unfolds over time. It happens gradually, and we develop a greater dependence on God and are strengthened in faith as we lean on Him throughout the process. When the temptation presents itself, He gives us the capacity in the moment to overcome it.

> In the world you will have tribulation; but be of good cheer, I have overcome the world.
>
> John 16:33

To be clear, prayer is a crucial and invaluable part of our lives. Prayer works, but how it works may be different from what we think. Prayer sensitizes our spirit and enables us to hear clearly the voice of our Counselor instructing us in the way we should go. Prayer helps us decipher which way to turn when we come to a fork—whether it is the fork in the road or the fork in our hand. It is what we do in that moment, at the choice point, that changes our direction. Prayer makes us sensitive in that moment. I recognized that God was not going to do it for me; He was going to do it *with* me. We were embarking on a journey together, with Him directing the way, and He would be "a lamp to my feet and a light to my path" as promised in Psalm 119:105. Our first step—and first stop: dealing with feelings.

4

Feelings: Friend or Foe?

> The best and most beautiful things
> cannot be seen or even touched.
> They must be felt with the heart.
>
> Helen Keller

We are built to feel. Jesus came that we might have life and life more abundantly (see John 10:10). Abundant life means experiencing all there is to experience to the fullest. Whether we admit it to ourselves or not, deep down we all desire larger-than-life emotional experiences, because when we feel deeply we feel alive. That is one reason we love falling in love. Love connects us to the depth of our emotions in a way we do not regularly access in the day-in, day-out routine of everyday life. It is like our soul shifts out of a dormant, neutral gear and into drive. In other words, our soul comes alive. Music and art can have the same effect. A beautiful song, a great book or a well-made film each have the capacity to take us into the core of who we are, and we find ourselves awakened and with a renewed zeal for life.

The desire for this experience is universal, which is why hundreds of strangers sitting in a dark movie theater can unite in a simultaneous experience of joy, laughter or tears. I have found that there are few things quite like a movie to not only connect us en masse, but personally to ourselves. The movies I love most are the ones that *move* me the most. Instead of being called a movie, it could be called a "move me" because that is what the really good ones do. I have exited many a theater, after crying my eyes out, feeling transformed and reconnected with the essence of who I am as a human being—walking through the world with a newfound awareness and sensitivity within myself and toward everything and everyone around me. Ah, it is good to feel alive! I love this experience and I am grateful for this gift granted through an inspiring film.

Why is that? Why can we have some of our most powerful experiences of being alive while watching the lives of others on-screen? Have you ever thought about why an actress like Julia Roberts earns twenty million dollars a picture? It is not merely because she is charming and pretty. There are thousands of charismatic and beautiful actresses in the world. She gets paid that amount because she is one of a select handful of actresses who are able to be so vulnerable, transparent and raw on-screen, that when she is feeling something, we are able to feel right along with her. We love that about her. We love her connection to her emotions, and we love how we connect with our emotions when we watch her. So, why do we allow ourselves to feel so deeply, yet vicariously, through actors playing a part on-screen, but in our own lives we resist our emotions and work overtime to keep them at bay?

In many ways feelings have gotten a bad rap. Even in church we are often taught that feelings are the enemy of faith, and in some ways that is true. We should not base all of our decisions solely on how we feel, because feelings fluctuate; they ebb and flow and are ever changing. However, living by our feelings and pretending feelings do not exist are two very different things. Many people think the way to stay in faith is to try to ignore negative feelings, but when we build a wall to block out certain negative feelings, that same wall barricades us from positive feelings, too.

Most of us embrace what we deem as positive, "godly" feelings like love and joy, but negate the negative emotions, such as anger and grief. Yet Scripture reveals that the Father, the Son and the Holy Spirit experienced the full range of emotions, and not just the "good" ones. God the Father was angry, Jesus wept and the Holy Spirit grieved. If it is okay for God Himself to feel, and we are made in the image and likeness of God, then it must be acceptable for us to feel all of our emotions as well.

When we shut ourselves off from negative feelings, we also close ourselves off from all feelings. That is why we walk around numb and half asleep in our lives. A wall around our hearts might seem to protect us from getting hurt, but it also shields us from experiencing the fullness of life that God has for us. The Bible does not teach us to suppress our negative feelings. It does not say do not be angry; rather, the Bible instructs us like this:

Be angry, and do not sin.

Ephesians 4:26

Feelings are not sinful, and we do not have to be ashamed of them either. Feelings themselves are not the problem. What we do with them, how we respond to them and where we allow them to take us is vital for our abundant life. Feelings are a driving force. They can take us on a ride, but where they take us is up to us.

I was having coffee by the beach one afternoon with a girl-friend who is an avid surfer. We were chatting about what it takes to confront our feelings and how the only way *to* is *through*. She got excited by the idea of dealing with emotions this way because she uses this identical principle to excel in surfing.

The first step of surfing is lying on your stomach on the surfboard and paddling out past where the waves are break-ing. Then you can settle back and wait for the perfect wave to ride in. But getting past the break is not easy; it can take some chutzpah to get out there. As you swim out, waves come at you in rapid succession, making it almost impossible to time your paddle out properly and navigate your way through. As a huge wave heads your way, about to crash on top of you, the natural instinct is to freeze in fear, or to hightail it in the other direction as quickly as possible. However, if you take either of those options, the wave will pummel you, and it will hurt. The best way to get to the other side of a breaking wave is to actu-ally swim as hard and as fast as you can directly *into* the face of the wave. The momentum will either get you up and over the wave, or it will help you to go right through the middle of the wave and come out unscathed.

In surfing, like in life, the only way to is through. Feelings are a driving force, but where they drive us is up to us. Like riding a wave, we can use our feelings to take a ride of escape into a counterfeit comfort, or to take a ride inward into the depths of ourselves. Strong feelings, like waves, are ominous and threatening. They can be scary and they have the potential to hurt us if we do not know how to handle them. Running from them is not the solution. If we do they will wind up over-taking us in the end. We can retrain ourselves to reject our natural instinct to protect ourselves by using avoidance and counterfeit comforts. We must be willing to face our feelings head on by purposefully going right into the middle of them.

Deliberately pushing into your pain is not natural. One of my favorite scenes in the movie *Million Dollar Baby* epitomizes this phenomenon. The main character, played by Hilary Swank, is training to become a professional boxer under the tutelage of her trainer, played by Clint Eastwood. Morgan Freeman plays Clint's partner and works with him at the gym. In one scene, Morgan is narrating about the life of a boxer and how unnatural it is. In a gentle, yet unshakable tone, Mr. Freeman says, in a way that only he can, "Boxing is an unnatural act, 'cause everything in it is backwards. You want to move to the left, you don't step left—you push on the right toe. To move right, you use your left toe. Instead of running from the pain, like a sane person would do, you step into it."

That scene resonated with me and reminded me of my teenage years spent training to become a professional dancer. Dancing is about retraining your body to move in a way that is counterintuitive. There is nothing natural about being able to kick your leg up right nexvt to your head. I do not ever remember walking down the street and saying, "Oh, look at that, my leg just accidently gravitated up toward my ear." Nope. It was hours and hours spent in the dance studio, retraining my muscles to move in a way contrary to how they moved naturally. It was weeks and months and years of undoing ingrained patterns and building new habits; repeating movements again and again until the unfamiliar became familiar and the familiar became unfamiliar.

We can use our feelings instead of our feelings using us.

Feelings are not our enemy. When we learn to embrace them, we recognize that they have great value to us, and we can use them instead of allowing them to use us.

God gave us feelings as indicators, signposts, to alert us that something inside of us needs attention. An intense, negative feeling or a strong emotional reaction to something often reflects a deep, unresolved issue. When we allow our feelings to be like waves that we ride into the innermost parts of who we are, we are able to discover what is behind the feelings, i.e., the roots. When we go to the root and deal on an emotional and spiritual level with God, then we can receive deep and lasting healing. The key here is *with* God. We need the Lord to reveal the hidden and secret places, and He does that as we learn to enter into those places with Him.

> Behold, I stand at the door and knock. If anyone hears My voice and opens the door, I will come in to him and dine with him, and he with Me.
>
> Revelation 3:20

He desires this kind of fellowship and intimacy with us. He is knocking, but God is a gentleman; He will not force His way in. It is up to us to open the door and invite Him in.

> God enters by a private door into every individual.
>
> Ralph Waldo Emerson

5

X Marks the Spot

Beware of the barrenness of a busy life.

Socrates

*E*veryday life is not conducive to getting into an intimate space with ourselves and with the Lord, because in order to do that, we have to remove ourselves from life's hurried pace. It takes getting quiet and still, and that is no easy feat nowadays. Most of us are busy, busy, busy, doing, doing, doing, and constantly on the go with our calendars scheduled down to the minute. We are also on our cell phones like never before. I see people walking across the street with their heads down and phones stuck to their ears. We cannot even sit in a waiting room for five minutes without our noses in our cells, sending an email or shooting someone a text. Distractions and the tasks of everyday life are detriments to our Christian walk. They hinder us from moving forward in God and getting where we truly want to be.

41

And the cares of this world, the deceitfulness of riches, and the desires for other things entering in choke the word, and it becomes unfruitful.

Mark 4:19

The "cares of this world" means life—running here and there, doing this and that. When we are too busy doing life's "stuff," the Word cannot go deep; therefore, we cannot get "into the deep" ourselves and become fruitful. Is life merely waking up, cooking food, cleaning dishes, running errands, cooking more food, cleaning more dishes, making phone calls, and then once again making more food and cleaning more dishes? Of course, we all have matters that demand our time and attention. We have work to do and family to care for, but most of us are in the business of busyness as if it is our full-time job. We need to see that busyness is a trap to keep us from entering into an intimate place with the Lord. Slowing down and getting quiet is the beginning of getting to know God.

Be still, and know that I am God.

Psalm 46:10

How difficult it is to resist the lure of constant activity. One day, some uncomfortable emotions were stirring within me. I was not sure what was up, but the last thing I wanted to do was sit in the discomfort. Choice point: Do I pray and get into God's presence, or do I keep moving in hope that busyness will help me to shake it off? I opted for the latter and headed to the gym. At my gym the treadmills are in a line facing a mirror. I hopped on the treadmill and started to walk. After a minute or two, I broke into a slow jog. As I was jogging I made eye contact with myself in the mirror. All of a sudden the Lord started speaking to me. I have to tell you, God is not religious. He will talk to us at obscure times and in various ways, some of them completely unconventional! So there on the treadmill I heard the Holy Spirit speak to my spirit. He said, "Look, there you are." I hit the acceleration button on the treadmill and ran faster. Again as I glanced at myself in the mirror, I heard, "Look, there you are." I upped my pace to a sprint. Running as fast as I could, I peeked hesitantly once again into the mirror and once again I heard, "Look, there you are."

Then I understood. The Holy Spirit was saying to me, "No matter how fast you run, you are still right there. You cannot out run yourself. Eventually you have to stop, be present and deal."

Stop, be present and deal? The very idea might be foreign to you. You may be thinking, *Where do I even start with this?* The place to start . . . is at the start. Identifying

> **To get where you are going, you have to know where you are.**

where you *are* makes it possible to navigate the path to where you want to go. Think of it like this: You are in the mall, trying to find a specific store. The first thing you do is go to the big directory board and locate the shop you want. Once you have spotted your destination, the next step is to figure out where you currently are. You ascertain that by finding that big red X on the map that says, "You Are Here." X marks the spot. Many of us have an idea of where we want to go, but we have no idea how to move toward getting there, because we are not clear about where we are.

We start by getting still. Journaling is an excellent way to inaugurate the journey inward. Instead of just going through our day haphazardly and with no intent, journaling can be a tool that assists us in reflecting upon our day and connecting with where we are in a more personal way. The word *journal* derives from the French word *jour*, which means "a day," so journaling is about logging our experiences *du jour* or "of the day." It can be much more than a log of events and activities, however. Journaling is a time to uncover and discover, to sink beneath the day-in, day-out routine of life to still ourselves and ponder. There is no right or wrong way to journal. It is a time for exploration, not judgment. Just get quiet and start writing.

I have found that posing questions to myself is a great way to get the process started. What do we do when we meet someone and want to get to know them? We ask questions. The better the questions the more we draw the other person out. We do not have to save our questions for other people, however. We can ask ourselves questions to begin to draw ourselves out.

The first question I ask myself is, *Where am I?* Not physically, but emotionally. It is like taking your emotional temperature. Where am I inside myself right now? Do I feel frazzled, anxious or uneasy? Do I feel negative, angry or frustrated? You want to pinpoint adjectives that describe your current state, such as tormented, peaceful, fearful or numb. If you find that you feel nothing or feel numb, then there is an opportunity to see if you can go deeper and expose what is behind the nothingness. Feeling nothing or feeling numb is a wall that is protecting something. If you are in that state, then most likely there is a lot more going on beneath the surface. Delve in.

Uncover what is undercover.

As you write, be aware of holding back on some level for fear that someone else will read your writing. This journal is for your eyes only. Find freedom within the pages to say, write or scribble whatever you like. Every time you hit a wall might be an opportunity to ask yourself another question to take yourself deeper. For example, *I feel frustrated. Why? Ah, it's because my spouse just snapped at me.* Continue investigating by asking yourself, "Why does that upset me?" More understanding will come, and the Holy Spirit will give you insight as you work through the process. Continue to check in with yourself to monitor where you are emotionally and physically: Is it hard to be still both literally and internally? Is my mind racing? Am I at peace? If not, then why not? What is tormenting me? What am I worried about? Can I identify exactly what happened—what was said or not said—that made me uncomfortable? What do I do when I'm uncomfortable? Do I eat, shop or watch television? What do I turn to for counterfeit comfort? How frequently do I run to these behaviors? Are they controlling me? How often do I eat when I'm not hungry or frantically clean the house even though it is already clean?

Through this process of discovery you will begin to recognize patterns and associations that trigger your counterfeit comfort behavior. Allow one question to beget another to gently guide you deeper into the discovery process. It takes time, patience and tenacity for many of us to begin to connect with where we are emotionally because we spend so much of our life with an external focus; we are always busy and moving. It takes practice to shift gears, and these kinds of questions will propel you into thinking about things and having realizations you have never had. That can be scary, but it is good. Beginning to identify where you are and what you are feeling is the first step, but it is only the beginning. While it takes time and effort, it is imperative that we spend this time exploring who we are and why we do what we do. Awareness is the first step to change. How can we change what we do not know?

You must know yourself to grow yourself.

John Maxwell

I want to know myself more fully, and like many Christians I have encountered, I long to know God on a greater level, but how? Knowing ourselves and connecting with ourselves connects us more deeply to God. Knowing God and connecting with God connects us more deeply with ourselves. Feelings can be the bridge we travel on between the two. Instead of stuffing our emotions or allowing them to drive us into our counterfeit comforts, we use our feelings to draw us into deeper intimacy with God and ourselves.

When I began this process I knew what I was supposed to do. I had all the "right" Christian answers. When I was uncomfortable, I was supposed to *give it to God, trust Him, surrender all, abide in the vine, focus on the cross of Christ and cast my cares onto Him.* Yeah, I knew all that, and I wanted to do those things with all my heart, but the problem was I didn't know how. There are many Scriptures that have become catchphrases, but that are not broken down into how-to applications. The how-to takes a concept and makes it practical and tangible. How do I trust the Lord? How do I surrender all? What does that look like in real life? Does that mean to read the Word more or to pray more? I posed those same questions to the Lord. It was then that He informed me that I already had the answer. It was something I had learned back in the third grade.

6

Stop, Drop and Roll

Let it be your business every day, in the secrecy
of the inner chamber, to meet the holy God.
You will be repaid for the trouble it may cost
you. The reward will be sure and rich.

Andrew Murray

*g*experienced a flash in my mind that took me back to
when I was a little girl, sitting in elementary school at
my tiny desk with the chair attached. I was watching a
film on what to do in case of a fire. I remember how the video
took us through the process step-by-step: During a fire drill,
at the sound of the bell, stand up from your desk in a calm
manner. Next, line up at the classroom door, and follow the
teacher single file and silently through the halls. After that,
walk out of the school building and onto the grassy quad.
Finally, wait with your group until it is safe to return to the

classroom. However, if by chance you happened to catch on fire, the video was very clear: Do not run. Instead:

Stop, Drop and Roll

This is exactly what the Lord spoke to my spirit: *When you are "on fire," so to speak, and full of emotions, such as rejection, fear or anger, instead of running, I want you to Stop, Drop and Roll.* And with this illustration, the Lord walked me through the process step-by-step.

Stop

In this context, *stop* means "stopping yourself in the middle of strong emotions" before you run to those cookies or whatever your counterfeit comforter might be. By stopping the pattern of running to the counterfeit and interrupting the knee-jerk reaction of meeting our own needs, we begin to develop a new pattern of turning to the Lord for comfort. It is always faster and easier to meet our own needs, because when we turn to comforts that are tangible, relief can be instantaneous. It is a wholly different thing when we turn to a God we cannot see or physically touch. It takes practice to learn how to connect *with* Him and receive comfort *from* Him. Over time, He will become more real and tangible to us as we develop the habit of turning to Him and allowing Him to comfort us. To break a habit and instill a new one takes time and repetition. We are probably not going to get it right at first or do it perfectly every time. That is not even the goal. The intention is to practice, to get still and *stop*. The next step is to *drop*.

Drop

In this instance, *drop* means "to get off your feet and plop yourself into a chair or onto the couch." You can even drop to the floor and lie on your back. Assume any position you desire. What is important is getting still in a quiet place where you can slow yourself down, get out of the urgency and frantic state, and have the opportunity to enter into God's presence. I personally like to lie on my back smack down in the middle of the living room floor. Much of my healing has happened in that very position when I have made myself available before God. Now that we have *stopped* and *dropped,* the next step is to *roll.*

Roll

By *roll* I mean "to roll or cast your cares onto the Lord."

Casting the whole of your care [all your anxieties, all your worries, all your concerns, once and for all] on Him, for He cares for you affectionately and cares about you watchfully.

1 Peter 5:7 AMPC

Instead of trying to handle everything on our own and in our own strength, this is the time to roll our cares and our worries over to Him, and allow Him to carry them for us. Our shoulders are not meant to carry all the weight of the world and all the burdens of life. We are used to living independently from the Lord, taking care of ourselves and meeting our own needs, but we as believers were never intended to live like that. We were not designed to carry the cares. We have a Father who loves us and wants to help relieve us of all the cares of life. He will take them. He is equipped to take them. He wants to take them.

Jesus said, "Come to Me, all you who labor and are heavy laden, and I will give you rest. Take My yoke upon you and learn from Me, for I am gentle and lowly in heart, and you will find rest for your souls. For My yoke is easy and My burden is light."

Matthew 11:28–30

I used to think that once I was a Christian, I would automatically be burden free; that life would be easy and bad stuff would not happen to me anymore. It did not take long to recognize the fallacy of that belief, and the Bible confirms it.

Many are the afflictions of the righteous, but the LORD delivers him out of them all.

Psalm 34:19

Regardless of our faith, we all go through rough times, and being a Christian does not make us exempt from trials. We will experience hurts, betrayal, loss and pain just like the rest of the world. We will experience suffering along with everyone else. The difference is we have someplace to turn and Someone to turn to. Because we have the Lord, we do not have to be mired down by the experiences we go through. When we are able to express our feelings and cast our burdens onto the Lord, resentment, grief and bitterness cannot take root in us. We can experience deep emotions, move through those emotions and come out the other side. Then we can get up and go about our day and way unencumbered. This is how we are able to overcome what overcomes the world. We can go to God.

So what does it mean to cast our cares? Do I merely say, "Lord, I cast my cares on You"? That is part of it, but casting our cares is not a catchphrase; it is an interaction with God. *Casting my cares* is a fancy way of saying "expressing my heart," i.e., talking to Him, and getting what I am feeling off my chest. This means being real and transparent. We do not need to pray our most holy, flowery, full-of-faith prayers when we go to God. We do not have to try to muster up faith or holiness to talk to Him or to try to impress Him. There is no need to be on our best behavior in hopes of pleasing Him. We want to get in there and get real, to be honest with ourselves and with the Lord. This might seem a little scary. You might be thinking, *I can't do that. I can't tell God how I really feel. Some of it is not very pretty.* Guess what? This is God we are talking about. He knows everything. He knows what is in our hearts, so trying to mask the truth with Him is pointless. We cannot tell Him something that He does not already know, so we do not have to put on an act. He wants us to come to Him just as we are—the good, the bad and the ugly. We don't have to try to be perfect for God. God is perfect for us. And our feelings, even the not so lovely ones, are perfectly okay with Him.

It is natural for us to need to release emotions, but it is how we release them that makes the difference. Repressed feelings find their way to the surface through destructive avenues. We may, for example, explode in rage and harshness toward those closest to us, or we may hurt ourselves with food or alcohol. But casting our cares onto the Lord by rolling our burdens over to Him is the best way to release unaddressed emotion. Doing so ensures that the resulting behavior does not inflict damage on others or ourselves. This healthy release actually strengthens us; it gives *to* us rather than takes *from* us. We do not have to be nervous about exposing our true selves to the Lord. He will not judge us or point out our flaws. He wants us to go deep and be truthful, not only with Him, but with ourselves.

> Behold, You desire truth in the inward parts, and in the hidden part You will make me to know wisdom.
>
> Psalm 51:6

In order to have truth in the inward parts, we have to examine the inward parts of ourselves. When we are honest about what is really going on, He gives us wisdom and understanding about our lives. God already knows what is in our hearts, but there is something about *us* seeing what is there that promotes healing. We do not have to strive to change ourselves or struggle to be different or better. It is merely the *seeing* of it that starts

51

to change us. Identifying, acknowledging and casting our cares all ignite the process of releasing us from what is holding us back from entering into freedom and wholeness. David said, "Cast your burden on the LORD, and He shall sustain you; He shall never permit the righteous to be moved" (Psalm 55:22). David was transparent before the Lord. He laid it all out. He never tried to be holy or prim and proper. He shared exactly what he was feeling: the deep despair and grieving in his heart, his anger, frustration and all that troubled him. David got real, and therefore his relationship with God was real. He was close to the Lord because he communed and fellowshiped with the Lord. We can have this same level of relationship with the Lord. Really? Yes, we can. When we get still and give Him the opportunity to commune with us, He will. Coming before the Lord this way and disclosing what is really going on inside you is what intimacy is all about, and it is in these times that something amazing can transpire. This is where God Almighty, the Creator of all, can become personal to us. A real Person we can talk to and become close with.

The times I have spent on the floor crying out to God, connecting with Him and with myself, have been the most tremendous and intimate experiences with the Lord that I have had. As much as I love corporate church gatherings, my deepest healing has taken place at home, one-on-one, with just the Lord and me. I often hung out with Him lying flat on my back in the middle of my living room floor. I actually deemed it my "on-the-floor ministry" because that was where the Lord revealed the mysteries and hidden things of both Himself and myself to me. Who knew that I could meet God in my living room, and that so much could take place on-the-floor?

7

On-the-Floor

To fall in love with God is the greatest of all
romances; to seek Him the greatest adventure;
to find Him the greatest human achievement.

Augustine

There is a difference between head knowledge of God and experiential knowledge of God. I do not want to know *about* Him; I want to *know* Him. I do not want to read about Him in a book or hear others talk about the Lord; I want to hear His voice, feel His presence and experience Him for myself. I desire the same level of intimacy and connection with God that I want with my spouse. I do not want to read about my husband or have someone else tell me what he is like. I want to talk with him, listen to him, laugh with him, and for us to hang out together. I want an actual partner to walk with through life, someone with whom I can share the good times and the difficult times. I want a real relationship.

53

One of the church's favorite catchphrases about Christianity is "it's not religion, it's relationship." We Christians love to make this statement when trying to minister to others to convince them that the Lord is personal. But truth be told, how many of us actually have a personal relationship with the Lord? Just going to church is not having a relationship. Just reading the Bible is not having a relationship. Just listening to our pastor's sermon on Sunday morning is not having a relationship. A relationship is an exchange where two parties engage with one another.

Our Christian life, and what we know about the Lord, was never intended to be based solely on what we receive second-hand. Receiving from our pastor, watching a sermon on television or reading a book are all invaluable practices that promote growth in our spiritual lives, and we can glean much through the wisdom and experience of those who have gone before us. However, we do not want our entire understanding of our Lord to come through what others have experienced. Secondhand revelation is great, but I will not be satisfied with that making up my entire Christian life. I expect firsthand revelation directly from the Lord as well. I want my own experiences to stand upon. What we learn about promotes knowledge, but what we experience goes deep and forms what we believe. We are taught that God is our Father, our Friend, our Counselor and our Comforter, but do we experience Him in those ways?

One of the ways I began to experience the Lord and receive firsthand revelation was during my on-the-floor ministry times. Getting *on-the-floor* means "getting still and posturing yourself to spend time with the Lord and enter into His presence." On-the-floor does not have to literally be time spent on the floor. It has been for me, but it can also be in a chair, on your bed or wherever you feel comfortable and private. As a matter of fact, my husband and I were having lunch with a couple that we minister to, and the man had recently heard my *Counterfeit Comforts* audio teaching. Over lunch he shared that he had just had some on-the-floor time with the Lord, but he did it guy style. He said, "My on-the-floor is in my truck. For me it's not on-the-floor, but in my Ford." Ha! That cracked us up!

There is truly no formula to this. On-the-floor is where you can be private, quiet and connected to God, and if that is in your Ford, then so be it! So now that we know what on-the-floor time is, let's break down when to do it, and how to do it.

When to Get On-the-Floor

A great time to hit the floor is when you are smack in the middle of strong feelings, when what is stirring within you is intense and all you want to do is run to the counterfeit to escape. If you have the opportunity to stop, drop and roll right then, do it. If you are out of the house, or at work, take a few minutes, if at all possible, and go to the bathroom, your car or outside to sit on a bench. You might not be able to have a full-blown on-the-floor session then and there, but by taking a minute or two, you will begin to break the knee-jerk response of running to a counterfeit comfort. Maybe something comes up at work, and it pushes a button in an unusual way. You might say, *Wow, okay, that really triggered me. I can't deal with it right now, but as soon as I get home from work, I'll resume right here. I'll get on-the-floor and deal with this then.*

You do not always need to experience extreme emotions to get on-the-floor. Maybe you are just kind of sad, a little down or sort of blah. There is a deeper, stronger feeling behind those subtle emotions. There is always a root. So even if you are just a bit off and not sure why, time in His presence on-the-floor can help you identify *why* you are feeling *what* you are feeling.

Another way to confirm that it is time to get on-the-floor is when you find yourself in the middle of counterfeit comfort activity or you have just completed counterfeit comfort activity. For instance, you could be right in the middle of binge eating, or cutting yourself, or you just finished an online shopping spree that you cannot afford. You might have no idea what you are feeling or that you are even having any feelings. The fact that you are in the middle of a counterfeit comfort should alert you that something is going on. It might be buried so deeply that you are not even aware of it. That is a good time to stop, drop and roll to investigate what is going on inside of you. The Holy Spirit will help you identify what you are feeling and what drove you to the counterfeit comforter. This can be tough. It is not often easy to halt a pattern when you are in the middle of it. Getting still and going inside will be extremely unfamiliar and probably uncomfortable. This might be the last thing you want to do. We are not conditioned to confront our feelings, so recognize that getting on-the-floor will most likely be a struggle at first and not what you are naturally inclined to do. Push through to the best of your ability, even if you start with giving God just one minute. The first hurdle is stopping and giving Him that time.

After completing counterfeit comfort behavior, you might be feeling too guilty or ashamed to want to look at anything. That is okay. With practice, you will find that you *will* be able to do this. There will come a time when, right in the middle of a counterfeit comfort, you will stop yourself and say, "I am not going to do this," and you will cry out to God right then and there.

We retrain ourselves to turn to our true Comforter, the Holy Spirit, instead of the counterfeit by building a habit of spending intimate time with the Lord. A great way to instill this new behavior is practicing on-the-floor time when you are feeling neutral. Neutral, meaning a time when you are not feeling anything in particular and there is no pressure to escape or act out. It is similar to deciding to have some prayer time—there is no urgent reason, just a desire to fellowship. When you do this, you are purposefully choosing to set time apart to connect with the Lord and practice entering into His presence. This begins to establish the healthy practice of learning to hear God's voice and opening your heart to self-exploration and discovery of what makes you, you. Spending time on-the-floor during emotionally balanced times develops a new pattern of turning to God. Then during those challenging times, when emotions are flaring and you really need it, the habit of turning to the Lord is formed and familiar and much easier to draw upon.

I remember when the Lord was fashioning this new behavior in me. He spoke to my spirit, "Just give Me five minutes. Come to Me; give Me a chance. If after that five minutes you still want a cookie, then get up and have it." I would want to binge so badly, but getting myself to stop and give God a moment began to break my pattern of instantly running to food, my most prominent counterfeit. Many times all it took was a decision of the will to interrupt the cycle by making the choice to take a few minutes and ask the Lord to help me discern what was really going on with me. Often after that time with Him, I would feel better. I would shift emotionally, and I would no longer feel the desire to continue down the road of destruction. Other times I would give God a few minutes and feel no differently. I would get up from the floor and eat, but even when that happened, I sensed the Lord's gentle touch guiding me emotionally, dissuading me from feeling guilty. He reassured me that I had not failed, as I thought I had, but by making the effort, I was building a new habit. I might not be successful every time, but over time, a new pattern would emerge, and I would see the difference.

So when is a good time for an on-the-floor ministry? Anytime is a good time to be with the Lord. There is never a bad time to separate yourself and get quiet before Him, and the time you spend will always be beneficial.

Now that we have covered *when* to have on-the-floor ministry time, let's break down what being on-the-floor looks like, and what to do once you get there.

What to Do On-the-Floor

There is no right or wrong way to be on-the-floor. This time is about connecting with the Person of the Holy Spirit, so your time with Him will be different each time. There is no formula or checklist on how to do it, but here is a loose guideline to assist you in navigating your way into the presence of the Lord and some simple, tangible how-to instructions.

Begin with a deep breath and say something along the lines of, "Okay, Lord, here I am; meet me here. Holy Spirit, help me to identify what I'm feeling right now."

As thoughts come to mind, do not question them or second-guess yourself, wondering if what you are thinking is really God or not. Often, the first thought that pops up is from the Holy Spirit. Go with the very first thing you receive. For example, you might think, *I feel sad.* Now you are on your way. Delve into it a bit. See if you can get more descriptive and specific. Maybe you sense more, such as *I feel sad, I feel rejected, unloved and alone.*

From here you want to go another level deeper. The way to do this is to continue to ask yourself and the Lord questions such as, "Okay, Lord, show me where this came from. What set me off today?" Ask the Holy Spirit to reveal what event triggered the emotion. "What upset me?" Be still for a moment, and allow the Lord to bring a thought or a picture to you. Maybe your friend walked by you at church and did not say hello. Perhaps your husband did not call to check in all day. It could be that your boss had some strong words for you. Whatever it is, do not judge it with thoughts like, *That's no big deal, I'm such a baby. That's nothing to be upset over.*

This is not the time to judge. Judgment halts the flow. Choose to accept whatever comes up from the biggest thing to the smallest. The key is making *everything* okay, valuable and worthwhile. If you are feeling something, then it is important and valid. Maybe others have judged your feelings in the past. You probably have, too. But God does not judge them, and in order for us to connect with ourselves, we have to make room for what we feel. We must receive ourselves completely. So when those thoughts of "this is so stupid, or petty or I'm being such a big baby" come up, tell those thoughts to shush. Choose to make your feelings about whatever happened okay. This is an opportunity to accept what you are feeling. Give the emotion room to breathe.

From this point on be like the surfer paddling directly into the face of the wave and purposefully propel yourself into the depths of the feeling, if possible. Get into the middle of it by choice, and instead of resisting, try to experience it. See if you can push into the feeling and explore it. You may cry as you begin to connect with the emotion in a visceral way. Do not hold back or temper yourself. This is not the time to try to be strong for yourself or your family or for God. Let the feelings loose. Let the tears flow.

For some, it will be easy to connect emotionally, while for others it will not come as naturally. Please hear this: There is no right or wrong way. Each one of us is unique. Some of us, because of painful experiences, have constructed such a solid fortress of protection around our hearts that it might take quite a while to crack that wall and begin to reconnect. If you do not have a strong emotional connection or any feelings at all that is absolutely okay. There is nothing wrong with you, and you are not doing it wrong. Try not to judge yourself or this process, merely recognize and observe. You might find that, *Hmm, my feelings are really strong right now,* or *Hmm, I see the wall I have constructed to protect myself because I am not feeling a thing,* or *I actually enjoy feeling and connecting,* or *Feeling anything is the last thing I want to do.* Discover and acknowledge where you are. Identifying and recognizing is the first step toward healing.

From there you can go yet another level deeper. This is where we ask the Lord to show us the root. For example, it might be clear that you feel rejected and unloved because of something that happened that day. As you delve deeper, however, you will probably uncover that this is not the first time you have felt this way. Ask the Lord to show you where this might have originated. Wait quietly and open yourself to hear and receive from Him. The inception of rejection most likely started long ago, instigated by events from childhood. As the Lord reminds us of past situations and memories, the root begins to be unveiled, and we almost always recognize a pattern. Let me give you a hypothetical example so you can get an idea of how it might unfold.

A Hypothetical On-the-Floor:

You are on-the-floor feeling uncomfortable and wanting to run to a counterfeit, but not sure why. You ask the Holy Spirit to help you identify what you are feeling. Let's say, for example, that a scenario from work earlier that day pops into your mind. It was lunchtime and a few colleagues were heading out the door to a restaurant close by. You were standing right there, but no one invited you to join the group. You felt totally invisible, left out, ignored. In a word, you felt rejected. Now you have identified what you were feeling—rejection— and from where it came. In the moment after your colleagues left, you probably were not even aware of how deeply you had been affected. You just knew that as soon as it happened you had an unction to binge or act out with counterfeit comfort behavior. Now the Holy Spirit is revealing specifics to you. You are connecting the dots and moving on the journey inward.

After having identified the feeling, you begin to tap in to the rejection while lying there on-the-floor, and, surprisingly, the intensity is extreme. Maybe you are thinking, *I'm not fourteen years old. Why did that affect me so severely?* This would be what I call a punishment that does not fit the crime–type scenario, where the reaction is far greater than the situation warrants. You might recognize that the hurt you felt at work had less to do with not being invited to lunch, and more to do with something deeper. The situation triggered a deep wound, and now there is a root to identify. This is where you start to get to the good stuff. "Okay, Lord," you say, "show me why I reacted so strongly. What is really going on here? Reveal the root to me."

Wait on the Lord. Be still for a few moments. The Lord will begin to bring things to your mind. Go with the first thing that comes up without questioning or judging. Maybe a picture flashes across your mind of you as a little girl watching your dad playing with your little brother while you are on the side-lines. All of a sudden you remember that you always felt like your dad loved your brother more than you. They always did special things together and your dad rarely spent any one-on-one time with you. Maybe it was made clear to you that your dad always wanted a boy and was disappointed when you were born. This would be a root, a root of rejection where you felt overlooked and not special or cherished. Rejection is a deep wound, and the situation at work with your colleagues is probably not the first time you felt this familiar sting. You most likely have encountered numerous occasions over the course of your life when this pattern played itself out, and where various circumstances elicited this response in you. Not being invited to lunch by co-workers merely poked a tender bruise from a long-ago wound.

As the Lord uncovers these buried wounds and brings memories back to the forefront of your mind, do not be surprised if strong emotions accompany your thoughts. Give them room. Allow yourself to feel them. Let them out. What comes up might be deep and guttural. Do not try to restrain the emotion. Go with it. Let's say, for the sake of this example, that as the image of you as a young girl is brought to your memory, some deep sadness accompanies it. As you begin to cry, it might even feel like you have gone back in time. You are that little girl crying about her daddy, and feeling the depth of those emotions like it was yesterday. Seeing yourself little might release a well of sadness that has been buried for years. It is okay to grieve. This grief has to come up and out so that you can move through it.

Perhaps, all of a sudden, Scriptures come to mind, words about your father and mother forsaking you . . . yet you also recall God's promise never to leave you or forsake you (see Psalm 27:10 and Hebrews 13:5). That is the Holy Spirit talking, and hearing Him like that can be tremendously healing. This is where Scriptures you have read a hundred times before instantly become personal to you. Then the Lord might back up that Scripture by giving you a picture of your dad engaging with your brother while you are on the sidelines, and then you see Jesus standing next to you holding your little hand. With that image may come a sense that the Lord is telling you that He was right there beside you all along. You might hear a whisper in your heart from the Lord saying, *I love you. You are so sweet and beautiful and precious to Me.* He might tell you a little secret like, *Your dad might have wanted a son, but I wanted a daughter. I wanted YOU. I chose you and made you, and I love everything about you.*

These kinds of moments with the Lord transform us. God does not necessarily erase our memories of the past, but as He heals us, those wounds no longer have the same sting.

Therefore, if anyone is in Christ, he is a new creation; old things have passed away; behold, all things have become new.

2 Corinthians 5:17

After an encounter with the Lord, Scripture like this becomes real and not just words on a page. It is personal and has meaning far beyond what it did before you spent time on-the-floor and before the Lord Himself spoke it into your heart.

Now we come to the most valuable key step while on-the-floor. After we release emotions and pent-up hurts from the past, we can be left with a strange void. This is normal and to be expected. Old, familiar parts of us have just been let go, and though they were parts we desperately wanted to be rid of, we still feel loss. A piece of us is missing, and there is a hole where those feelings and hurts used to reside. This is where we ask the Lord to come in and fill that hole and flood us with His love. What I do is this: I take a deep breath and picture the love and the goodness of Jesus filling that empty space and my entire body. I breathe in His Spirit and healing balm like it is air. It actually helps to physically take deep breaths and visualize Him filling you as you do. I might say something like, "Lord, where I've had that wound of rejection, that place where I feel so unloved, touch me in that place, heal that wound, fill me with Your love." Then I take a deep breath in, imagining His love filling me as I inhale. *Lord, let me know what's true, that You love me, and allow me to feel Your love.* I take another deep breath, focusing on breathing in His love, and sensing it move throughout my body. I continue to breathe Him in and allow His love to fill every empty and wounded place. I might focus on opening my heart to Him by whispering something like,

"I receive. I receive. I receive Your love." To lie there and bask in His presence can be a very beautiful time. For some, this might open the door for you to have your first true experience of God's presence in a personal way.

So, how do you know when your on-the-floor session is done? There is no formula or precise format. Sometimes I am on-the-floor for a few minutes, sometimes a couple of hours. You will need to feel it out for yourself. Regardless of the time spent, it is always worth it. It is challenging to put an on-the-floor experience into words, because when we have a supernatural encounter with the Lord, we cannot always put our finger on exactly what transpired. Somehow we just know that something is different. Many times after being on-the-floor I knew something had happened between the Lord and me and that something inside me had shifted as a result. Where there had been despair, I felt peace. Where I had been hollow, I felt content. A knowing would come over me that something had been worked through, and for now I was done. I would get up off the floor, not as if I was 100 percent healed of every single thing I had ever gone through in my life, but as if a piece of the puzzle had been filled in. I was a step further along in the process of restoration, and it was happening one little piece at a time.

It hurts my heart knowing that God created us for intimacy with Him, yet many believers go their entire lives never feeling and hearing the Lord in this way. It is actually the most natural thing in the world. Unfortunately, most of us have never been taught how to truly know Him, feel Him, hear His voice or connect with His presence. The good news is, it is never too late. You can know Him like this now. He wants that. The on-the-floor experience is an opportunity to invite God the Healer to do what He does best: heal.

He heals the brokenhearted and binds up their wounds.

Psalm 147:3

O Lord my God, I cried out to You, and You healed me.

Psalm 30:2

When it comes to emotional healing, we mistakenly believe that it happens like the touch of a magic wand, and *poof* one day we are all better. I have found it to be a much more intricate process than that. Often the Lord takes us right into the middle of our wounds for us to really see what is there before He brings us out to the other side. Before we are healed it almost always seems like things are darker, harder and more extreme. We have to be willing to go through this process. It is much like birth. Birth is not neat and tidy—it is a little intense. Okay, more than a little, but we continue to push through, eagerly awaiting the promise of life on the other side.

A woman, when she is in labor, has sorrow because her hour has come; but as soon as she has given birth to the child, she no longer remembers the anguish, for joy that a human being has been born into the world.

John 16:21

When we prevail, the life awaiting us on the other side of labor is our own, and everything we endured to birth our newfound freedom was worth it.

8

My Personal Process

Higher heights require deeper depths.

Robia Scott

When Almighty God, Creator of the Universe, is allowed access into your life, and begins to talk to you about your life, absolutely nothing compares. One of my most pivotal seasons with the Lord took place over a few months and a number of hours on my living room floor. It was after He spoke to me about my counterfeit comforts that He began taking me through a healing transformation starting with this experience:

I was lying on-the-floor one day when the image of a tall, red brick building suddenly came to the forefront of my mind. You could tell that the building had been around for a while, as if it had some history to it. In the movie playing inside my head, a giant wrecking ball appeared and was beelining at rapid speed toward the center of the building. Upon impact, bricks became dust that fell to the ground, leaving a massive hole in the side of the structure. The building teetered, as if it could collapse at any moment. Just then, I realized that the building represented me, and I was being torn down. The Lord had given me a visual that was symbolic to the work He was doing inside of me.

As I reflected on this and what it meant, I sensed in my spirit that this was just the beginning. That not only was my building coming down, but my entire foundation was about to be uprooted as well. Then in a way that I could understand, the gentle voice of the Lord began to unfold for me what was about to take place in my life. He started speaking to me about my foundation. He said, "The problem is not your building. Your foundation is why your building is not secure. I need to uproot your foundation and lay a new one. Then I will be able to build upon it, so you will be solid; you will be steady; you will be planted on the rock. When trials come against you and when storms arise, you will not go down, but you will be able to endure." I felt peace in my heart because I knew what I was hearing aligned with Scripture (see Luke 6:47–48).

After the Lord impressed those words upon me I became curious about the correlation between laying a foundation in the spiritual and laying a foundation in the physical when creating an actual building. So, I decided to study it out a bit. Before building a structure, great care goes into planning the foundation prior to breaking ground. A proper foundation ensures the security of the entire building. Surveying is done first to learn if the land is level and stable enough to build upon. Then detailed calculations are made to determine exactly how much weight the building will hold, down to each desk, chair and computer, in order to ensure a foundation that can support the weight it must carry.

In both the natural realm and in the Lord, there is much preparation prior to the first brick being laid. It reminds me of this Scripture:

> But the word of the LORD was to them, "Precept upon precept . . . line upon line . . . here a little, there a little."
>
> Isaiah 28:13

Process—a little at a time, over time—is how the Lord builds us with His truth. Much like laying brick, He does it brick upon brick, line upon line, truth upon truth, until a strong structure is in place. The higher the building, the deeper you must dig the foundation in order to secure it. Just like in our Christian walk, the further in God you want to go, the higher you want to soar, and the freer you desire to be—to the same degree you want to go up, you must go deep.

How Far and How Deep?

This is where you might pause and ask yourself, *How far do I want to go in God? How deep am I willing to go? Am I willing to be uncomfortable and do whatever it takes to have everything available to me in the Lord?*

One more fascinating fact about foundations is that while incredibly solid, they are also designed to be somewhat flexible. They are made with some margin of give, so that the structure upon them is able to sway and shift. The foundation is specifically crafted to bend and not break as it encounters adverse elements, such as strong winds or an intense storm. As I read that, I recalled what the Lord had shown me on-the-floor and how many times I had prayed Luke chapter six over my life, how many times I had cried out to the Lord to make me the house on the rock, and not the sand.

69

Whoever comes to Me, and hears My sayings and does them, I
will show you whom he is like: He is like a man building a house,
who dug deep and laid the foundation on the rock. And when
the flood arose, the stream beat vehemently against that house,
and could not shake it, for it was founded on the rock. But he
who heard and did nothing is like a man who built a house on
the earth without a foundation (or "sand," see Matthew 7:26),
against which the stream beat vehemently; and immediately it
fell. And the ruin of that house was great.

Luke 6:47–49

All I desired was to be solid and steadfast; a house that could
not be shaken regardless of life's tribulations. Now God was
actually answering my prayers, but in a fashion that looked
nothing like I had anticipated. I had not expected this arduous process. I wanted to be different and new, but I thought
it would just happen in an instant.

Prayers of complete surrender sound nice in a worship song,
but being in the middle of it, living and walking it out, is an
entirely different matter. Surrendering "all" brings with it a
lot of uprooting and replanting, shifting and swirling before
resettling. The Lord promises that in Him we are each made
a new creation in Christ. Sounds great in theory. Who would
not want to become a new creation, a new building? We are all
for it, but rarely are we taught *how* we become a new creation
in Christ, the process that ensues, or all that it entails. What
would it mean to uproot my foundation? How would that look
and feel? The Holy Spirit began showing me that so much of
what I thought and believed, formed through my childhood
and various teaching and experiences, was incorrect. *Everything*
that contradicted the Word and the truth had to go.

Foundations are like the roots of a plant. The longer the
plant is in the ground, the more time the roots have to dig
in deep and anchor themselves. What it takes to uproot a

70

small garden plant is vastly different from pulling an old oak out from its roots. Many of us are more like that old oak because unresolved hurts from our past have had decades to take root. Those roots have anchored themselves in us and have formed what we think, how we feel and how we move through our lives.

When those troubled areas begin to be uprooted, it can get intense and messy. As a deeply rooted tree is pulled up, dirt and soil are upturned, and the entire area becomes disrupted. What remains is a big hole where a lovely tree used to be, and for a while, the ground looks pretty undone. It is the same with us emotionally. This is not to scare you, because the Lord will always be gentle with us, but we have to understand that it is probably going to be uncomfortable. God will comfort us through the discomfort, but it won't necessarily be neat and tidy. We are talking about a mighty move of God in our lives, a huge transformation of how we think, and a work done to realign us with who we truly are. This usually does not transpire with one prayer and a worship song.

I knew something deep, very deep, was taking place within me. The Lord started showing me situations from my past. In particular, dynamics that went down with my family that had established belief systems He needed to uproot. Memories and feelings were coming up that were not easy to revisit, but they were too true to be denied. I cried and cried until I felt all cried out. Then I experienced a weird sensation, as if something that had needed to go was now gone, as if a part of me was literally missing. And though it was good and right that it had gone, I felt the emptiness. There remained a big hole inside of me. I said out loud, "Lord, I don't know exactly what You are doing, but I feel so empty and strange, like a big blob of nothingness. How am I going to function, or do anything, or become anything, when I'm like this? I don't even know who

71

I am right now or how I feel. What's going to happen to me? I hope You don't leave me like this."

Before I finish that story, I need to fill you in on some history. Cut to twenty years earlier. When I was a young girl my favorite TV show was *The Bionic Woman*. I loved the lead character, Jaime Sommers, played by Lindsay Wagner. I loved her, loved her, *loved* her and wanted to be just like her. In fact, my best girlfriend and I would spend afternoons outside in the backyard reenacting *The Bionic Woman*. We would attempt to run in slow motion while simultaneously making the bionic woman's sound effects with our mouths: *b i y i y i y i y i*. We would jump in slow motion as much as humanly possible with adjoining sound effects: *b i y i y i y i y i*. My friend would call my name, "Hey, Robia!" I would turn toward her in slow motion . . . *b i y i y i* . . . letting her know that my bionic ear was picking up the vibration of her voice. We had hours of fun running through the neighborhood, pretending to be Jaime Sommers until the sun went down and it was time to go inside for dinner.

Now, cut back to where I had left off from my previous story. There I am lying on-the-floor feeling like I had been filleted open, emotionally vulnerable, nose running, and a huge pile of used tissues next to my head. I said, "Lord, what can You possibly do with me? I feel worthless. I don't know who I am, how I feel or where I'm going. I'm a big pile of nothingness." In between sniffles and wondering what would become of me, I heard in my spirit:

We can rebuild her. We have the technology.

What? Are you kidding me? The Lord was quoting *The Bionic Woman* to me? I had not thought about that show in years, and now the Lord was speaking to me using the opening line of the program, "We can rebuild her. We have the technology." *We* represented the Father, the Son and the Holy Spirit. *We* can rebuild her. In other words, *We* know how to do it, and restoration is *Our* area of expertise. *We* have the technology, the ability, the know-how and the desire.

That made me laugh out loud. So there I was, on-the-floor, laughing, crying and marveling at how funny and truly personal God is. Nothing had really changed as far as my circumstances were concerned. I was still as vulnerable as could be there on-the-floor, but in that moment I knew I would be okay. I knew He would not leave me in that interim stage. I knew I would make it to the other side, and that He would see me through until I arrived.

Even in the midst of the pain, and although what was going on inside of me was intense, and it hurt, there was something exhilarating about the process. It was scary, but at the same time enjoyable and exciting because I knew, that I knew, that I knew that God was doing something in me, and that it was good. I was having a life-changing experience on my floor with Almighty God. I felt as if I was beginning to know the Lord on a whole new level, and in the process, getting to know myself in a new way as well. It was as if the Lord was introducing *me* to me—who I truly was minus the junk. I was a newer Christian, so I asked a handful of people at church if they had ever been through something like this. No one knew what the heck I was talking about. I knew then that this was going to be something personal between the Lord and me. I also got a sense that this was available to everyone, but not everyone was willing to launch into the deep and to have the courage to invite God in as well. I knew that the Lord wanted all His children to trust Him enough to allow Him to take them into this level of depth, and that it was through this process that true healing would come.

I had entered into unfamiliar territory, not 100 percent sure of what I was doing. I chose to believe, though, that if I stayed close to the Lord, He would direct my steps, and as Scripture promises be "a lamp unto my feet, and a light unto my path" (Psalm 119:105 KJV). The Lord also backed up what He was doing in me by giving me Scriptures to stand on along the way so that I could be secure in knowing that what was happening was of Him. Just when I needed it, I came across this verse:

> Every plant which My heavenly Father has not planted will be uprooted.
>
> Matthew 15:13

That is exactly what was taking place in me. Everything planted in me that was not God—every thought, every belief system, everything contrary to the Word, everything that God had not planted—was being uprooted and replaced with truth, line upon line, precept upon precept, truth upon truth.

And then, in God's perfectly ordained timing, I came upon this Scripture:

> But now He has promised, saying, "Yet once more I shake not only the earth, but also heaven." Now this, "Yet once more," indicates the removal of those things that are being shaken, as of things that are made, that the things which cannot be shaken may remain."
>
> Hebrews 12:26–27

This is precisely what I had prayed for, and it was happening! I was being shaken to the core, so that what was in me that could be shaken was being removed, and what remained in me would be solid and steadfast. I almost could not believe it when I came across those Scriptures. It was as if they jumped off the page and right into my heart. The Holy Spirit was directing me, counseling me and speaking to me! I knew He had led me to those Scriptures to assure me that what I was experiencing was real and of Him. How the Lord used those verses to speak to me was a bit different from how they were used in the context of what He was saying in Matthew and in Hebrews. Yet at the same time, I knew that He was highlighting them for me personally. They were not verses out of context, but Scriptures He was using in the context of my life to confirm what He was doing in me.

I knew I was being shaken and transformed, but at moments I would question *The Bionic Woman* reference. *Did the Lord really speak that to me? Really? The Bionic Woman?* Months later, as I was reading in the book of Jeremiah, I came upon:

> Again I will build you, and you shall be rebuilt.
>
> Jeremiah 31:4

The Holy Spirit reminded me of what He had spoken to me on-the-floor: "We can rebuild her. We have the technology." I sat there staring at the Bible in shock and, again, had to laugh. I know all things originated with the Word, but who knew that *The Bionic Woman* actually began in Scripture? Ha! God is too good! Only He can perform such an intricate work while infusing humor at the same time. Ironically enough, I recently came across the following quote from the bionic woman herself:

> A lot of people say they want to get out of pain, and I'm sure that's true, but they aren't willing to make healing a high priority. They aren't willing to look inside to see the source of their pain in order to deal with it.
>
> Lindsay Wagner, Actress, *The Bionic Woman*

Sounds like a woman who has spent some time on-the-floor.

9

Do Not Believe
Everything You Think

The first step on the way to victory
is to recognize the enemy.

Corrie ten Boom

a number of issues will arise to derail your time on-the-floor. Be prepared for it. There are a handful of pitfalls that can, and most likely will, come up for you to be aware of and avoid. Numerous thoughts and circumstances will attempt to hinder you through your on-the-floor process, and some will come in to undo you before you even make it there. These tactics that derail you are called spiritual warfare. The enemy will attempt to block you at every turn. Yes, you have an enemy, an adversary, who is strategic in his attacks against you, but there is good news. Scripture teaches us strategies to overcome and defeat our adversary.

Let us get into how the enemy operates and expose some of his tactics, so you will know what to expect and how to prevail regardless of what comes against you. Laying this foundation will give you a greater understanding of the enemy and spiritual warfare, because if you are like many Christians, you have probably not had much teaching on this topic. As believers, we must realize that we are in a SPIRITUAL BATTLE. In Ephesians chapter six, the Bible tells us who and what we are wrestling:

> Finally, my brethren, be strong in the Lord and in the power of His might. Put on the whole armor of God, that you may be able to stand against the wiles of the devil. For we do not wrestle against flesh and blood, but against principalities, against powers, against the rulers of the darkness of this age, against spiritual hosts of wickedness in the heavenly places.
>
> Ephesians 6:10–12

What does "We do not wrestle against flesh and blood" mean? Our struggle is not actually with ourselves or with others, as much as we might think it is. We have all heard the saying, "I am my own worst enemy." Well, let me tell you something: You are not your own worst enemy. You are not your greatest obstacle. We have an adversary who is very real and out to destroy us, and that enemy is not ourselves. I repeat, you are not your own worst enemy. *The enemy is your own worst enemy.* Say that out loud, so it gets into your heart and spirit.

> *I am not my own worst enemy.*
> *The enemy is my own worst enemy.*

The apostle Paul relates our spiritual walk to a fight when he instructs us to "fight the good fight of faith" (1 Timothy 6:12).

By definition, *being in a fight* means you have an opponent. So if we are in a battle, and we are not fighting ourselves, then with whom are we fighting? We are in a fight with a thief, a murderer, a destroyer whose motive is to harm us in any way he can. That might sound extreme, but Jesus Himself warns us in His Word: "The thief does not come except to steal, and to kill, and to destroy. I have come that they may have life, and that they may have it more abundantly" (John 10:10). Jesus came to bring us life—prosperity in every way: health to our bodies, peace to our minds and joy in our hearts. But the enemy comes to steal those very things from us.

It is imperative to recognize that we have an enemy. He is real and his existence is scriptural. Many churches and Christians do *not* want to talk about the enemy. They adopt the mindset that verbalizing the existence of the enemy glorifies him, so it is better not to give him any attention. "Only focus on Christ," they say. This is a detrimental error. It is like jumping into shark-infested waters and saying, "Sharks, you do not exist to me. I'm not even going to look at you. I'm just going to 'focus on Jesus.'" You can imagine just how effective that plan would be! You can pretend the sharks are not there at all. You can act like they are not real and declare they do not exist, but you exist to those sharks. You are very real to them. They are keenly aware of your presence, and unless you have a plan, you will find yourself in serious trouble.

Simply instructing us as believers to "focus on Jesus" is not the way God equipped us to deal with spiritual warfare. Skilled combatants do not take such an approach when it comes to battle. Those in the military take studying their enemy very seriously. One of the most effective strategies in wartime is "know your enemy." In a memorable scene in the movie *Patton*, U.S. General George S. Patton has just spent weeks studying the writings of his German adversary, Field Marshall Erwin Rommel. Patton is crushing him in an epic tank battle in Tunisia. Patton, sensing victory as he peers through his binoculars onto the battlefield from his command post, says,

"Rommel, I read your book!" I love that! Patton did not go into battle just believing the best. He studied his opponent's strategies and used his adversary's own plan of action against him to defeat him. Patton beat his enemy at his own game. We must do the same.

We do not have to over-spiritualize this principle of knowing our enemy. Even in sports the strategy of focused study is applied. Football teams, tennis players, and in virtually every sport where one has an opponent, the team or player invests as much time watching videos of their opponent as they do in developing their own skills. Hours are spent studying their opponent's strengths and weaknesses in order to know what to expect and how to counter and defeat them.

When it comes to our Christian life we must understand that the battle we are in is serious. We are at war, and in war ignorance is not bliss—it is death. It is the same for us spiritually. Ignorance will destroy us. Acknowledging our enemy is not glorifying him. Understanding our opponent, and using the tools God has granted us is wisdom, not enemy glorification. No one wins a battle by hoping and wishing. A battle is won by knowledge, wisdom and understanding.

My people are destroyed for lack of knowledge.

Hosea 4:6

This is a major reason so many Christians are struggling and defeated. Not only are we unaware of the strategies of our enemy, but we have never been schooled in how to defeat him. We must learn our adversary's tactics in order to come out victorious.

There are a number of ways the enemy comes to steal from us and hurt us. It can be an attack on our health or on our finances, but one of the main ways we get attacked is in our thought realm.

The battle is in the mind.

Understanding this aspect is crucial to living an abundant life in Christ, but again, rarely taught. We are offered adverse thoughts and ideas from our enemy all day long. Our adversary talks to us in a way that is so subtle that we often do not recognize him as the source and we mistakenly accept his thoughts as truth. These thoughts enter in so seamlessly that, unless we are taught to look for them, we can easily miss the signs that they are coming from an outside source. And because we think and hear these wayward thoughts in first person, they sound as if they are our own. That is why we often look at ourselves as the problem.

For though we walk in the flesh, we do not war according to the flesh. For the weapons of our warfare are not carnal but mighty in God for pulling down strongholds, casting down arguments and every high thing that exalts itself against the knowledge of God, bringing every thought into captivity to the obedience of Christ.

2 Corinthians 10:3–5

This is such a pivotal Scripture, that it is a good idea to look it up in various translations so that it can be fully understood.

For though we live in the world, we do not wage war as the world does. The weapons we fight with are not the weapons of the world. On the contrary, they have divine power to demolish strongholds. We demolish arguments and every pretension that sets itself up against the knowledge of God, and we take captive every thought to make it obedient to Christ.

NIV

For though we walk (live) in the flesh, we are not carrying on our warfare according to the flesh and using mere human

81

weapons. For the weapons of our warfare are not physical [weapons of flesh and blood], but they are mighty before God for the overthrow and destruction of strongholds, [Inasmuch as we] refute arguments and theories and reasonings and every proud and lofty thing that sets itself up against the [true] knowledge of God; and we lead every thought and purpose away captive into the obedience of Christ (the Messiah, the Anointed One).

AMPC

Paul states that although we live in the world (the realm of Satan's influence) and in the flesh (the part of us alienated from God), we do not battle using "mere human weapons." Instead, Paul teaches us that our plan in battle is to "demolish strongholds." A stronghold is a negative mindset. A thought your mind adheres to strongly. Strongholds are thoughts given to us by the enemy so often that they form a pattern or groove of thinking that becomes our default. Our objective is to destroy these strongholds, but how? We are taught that in order to demolish strongholds we must "cast down arguments." All three versions of this Scripture use the word *arguments* in verse five. An argument consists of two parties with opposing views and positions vying for their perspective to dominate. That is exactly what is going on in the spirit realm: There is an argument going on in our mind between lies and truth. Our arguments are wrong thoughts, wrong ideas and wrong feelings being given to us from the wrong source.

In Scripture, Satan is called "the father of lies."

You belong to your father, the devil, and you want to carry out your father's desires. He was a murderer from the beginning, not holding to the truth, for there is no truth in him. When he lies, he speaks his native language, for he is a liar and the father of lies.

John 8:44 NIV

That is what our adversary does: He tells lies. It is his job, and he is the best at it. Jesus is the King of kings, and Satan is the king of deception. There is a war being waged over what we will think and what we will believe. All day long we are given the opportunity to do one of two things: believe in and think upon thoughts that are from God, or believe in and think upon thoughts from the enemy. It is our job to discern those thoughts and lies that are trying to "exalt themselves" over the truth of the Word in our minds. We must purposefully resist, reject and cast out those thoughts. We have to refuse them—say "No!" to them. What we don't realize is that by allowing and accepting such thoughts, we are coming into agreement with them.

> Again I say to you that if two of you agree on earth concerning anything that they ask, it will be done for them by My Father in heaven.
>
> Matthew 18:19

If we pray in agreement and in unity then what we ask will be done. The principle here is when two agree there is power, it cements what is agreed upon and brings it to fruition. There is power in agreement. This Scripture is often taught regarding agreement with another person, and that is accurate, but let's take it to another level. All day long we are agreeing with something in the spiritual realm. Who and what are we agreeing with? Are we agreeing with God and His truths or with an enemy who is continually offering us thoughts and ideas that are contrary to God's thoughts and ideas? Jesus taught us about the voice of the enemy, when He said, "The sheep follow him, for they know his voice. Yet they will by no means follow a stranger, but will flee from him, for they do not know the voice of strangers" (John 10:4–5).

None of us as believers purposefully choose to follow the voice of the stranger. However, many of us do so unknowingly because we have not been taught how to differentiate between the voice of the Lord and the voice of the enemy. So how do we discern between? One way to identify something is by its sound. For instance, we know a cat is a cat because it says *meow*. We know a dog is a dog because it says *woof! woof!* That is a simplistic concept, but actually perfect for beginning to discern between God and the enemy.

God has a sound and a tone, and so does the enemy. There is a tone behind certain thoughts we think. They are either uplifting (God), or critical and harsh (enemy). What do you think the enemy might sound like in everyday life? Do you ever have thoughts like these?

- *I can't do anything right. Why bother even trying?*
- *My prayers are dumb. I feel stupid praying. I don't even know what to say.*
- *I hope God's not mad at me.*
- *No matter what I do, I don't think I'm pleasing God.*
- *I wonder what I did wrong to deserve this.*
- *I'm fat. I'm ugly. I hate myself. I hate my life.*
- *I should just kill myself.*
- *What's wrong with me?*

You probably identify with at least one, if not all, of the thoughts on that list. Most of us have no idea that these are signs of spiritual warfare. Thoughts like these are not our own thoughts. Did you catch that? I repeat: Thoughts like these are *not* our own thoughts. They feel so natural, and so normal, that we get duped into believing that they are our thoughts. They flow through our mind in the first-person form, and in such a seamless fashion, that it is almost imperceptible that they are coming from an outside source. We think they are our own, and that is how we are deceived.

It is easy to waste time and energy trying to discern if certain thoughts originated with you or the enemy. That is another of the enemy's tactics to get your mind reeling and swirl you into a ball of confusion. Don't take the bait. For now, keep it simple. If the thoughts are negative, self-deprecating or do not line up with God's Word, you do not want them. You do not want to think on them, receive them, accept them or believe them.

One clue that a thought is from the enemy is if the tone behind the thought is accusatory:

> For the accuser of our brethren, who accused them before our God day and night, has been cast down.
>
> Revelation 12:10

The enemy, our adversary, is an accuser. He blames and finds fault in everything we do, and then taunts us with it. Our Father does not talk to us like that. Once we identify the difference, we no longer have to receive what the enemy gives us. The good news is that we have dominion over the thoughts in our minds. We can resist those thoughts.

Peter instructs us wisely:

> Be sober, be vigilant; because your adversary the devil walks about like a roaring lion, seeking whom he may devour. Resist him.
>
> 1 Peter 5:8–9

We resist the enemy by rejecting and casting down the thoughts he gives us. He has the intent to steal, kill and destroy us. Let that be what you remember as you are on guard against his harmful, condemning thoughts. We cannot resist what we do not know, but now we know: We have dominion over the thoughts of our mind. We can resist those thoughts. We can get free.

Never give in, never, never, never—in nothing great or small, large or petty—never give in except to convictions of honour and good sense. Never yield to a force; never yield to the apparently overwhelming might of the enemy.

Winston Churchill

10

The Sound of God

The spiritual life is a life in which you gradually
learn to listen to a voice that says something else,
that says, "You are the beloved and on you my
favor rests." I want you to hear that voice. It is not
a very loud voice because it is an intimate voice. It
comes from a very deep place. It is soft and gentle.
I want you to gradually hear that voice. We both
have to hear that voice and to claim for ourselves
that that voice speaks the truth, our truth. It tells us
who we are. That is where the spiritual life starts—
by claiming the voice that calls us the beloved.

Henri J. M. Nouwen

Once we discern the difference between the sound of
God and the sound of the enemy, we become em-
powered. We are free to choose, free to receive only
thoughts that are from God; thoughts with the right tone that
are from the right Spirit, the Holy Spirit. Now that we have

familiarized ourselves with the kinds of thoughts the enemy gives us, let's learn how to identify God thoughts.

God thoughts sound like this:

- I love you.
- You are special to Me.
- You can do it.
- I believe in you.
- Don't give up.
- I have not given up on you.
- I have a plan for your life, and it is good.
- Everything is going to be all right.
- You are perfect in My sight. That's right, I said perfect.
- You are pleasing to Me because of who you are, not because of what you do.
- Even if you make mistakes, I love you.
- You have not blown it.
- You are wonderful.

You might be thinking that all of this sounds like a bunch of gushy, mushy, wishful thinking. How do we know that this is how God sounds? We go to the Word. Every one of those statements is scriptural, and here is the proof:

- *I love you.* "For God so loved the world that He gave His only begotten Son" (John 3:16).
- *You are special to Me.* "But you are a chosen generation, a royal priesthood, a holy nation, His own special people, that you may proclaim the praises of Him who called you out of darkness into His marvelous light" (1 Peter 2:9).
- *You can do it. I believe in you. Don't give up.* "And let us not grow weary while doing good, for in due season we shall reap if we do not lose heart" (Galatians 6:9).

88

- *I have not given up on you. I have a plan for your life, and it is good.* "I know the thoughts that I think toward you, says the LORD, thoughts of peace and not of evil, to give you a future and a hope" (Jeremiah 29:11).
- *Everything is going to be all right.* "And we know that all things work together for good to those who love God, to those who are the called according to His purpose" (Romans 8:28).
- *You are perfect in My sight. That's right, I said perfect. You are pleasing to Me because of who you are, not what you do.* "For He made Him who knew no sin to be sin for us, that we might become the righteousness of God in Him" (2 Corinthians 5:21).
- *Even if you make mistakes, I love you. You have not blown it.* "For a righteous man may fall seven times and rise again" (Proverbs 24:16).
- *You are wonderful.* "For You formed my inward parts; You covered me in my mother's womb. I will praise You, for I am fearfully and wonderfully made; marvelous are Your works, and that my soul knows very well" (Psalm 139:13–14).

For some of you, learning that this is how God speaks to us is like a cool drink of water, refreshing to your soul. To others, this might be so unfamiliar that every part of your being is squirming right now, and you are having trouble believing that this is actually how God thinks about you and how He talks to His children. I am not making this up to be a Pollyanna or a super-saccharine Suzie Christian. This is the Bible—the infallible Word of God. It is the absolute, irrefutable truth. Period. God is love, and the spirit and tone behind His words are always uplifting. He is never critical or harsh EVER.

What about when God is correcting us or chastening us? Wouldn't He be harsh then? The Bible does say the Father chastens those He loves.

> For whom the LORD loves He chastens.
>
> Hebrews 12:6

The Lord can be very strong when He corrects us, but it is never through condemnation. God does not speak in a condemning fashion EVER. There is a big difference between conviction from the Lord and condemnation from the enemy. When you are feeling guilty and condemned, that is not God's voice correcting you. How do we know? It is scriptural:

> There is therefore now no condemnation to those who are in Christ Jesus, who do not walk according to the flesh, but according to the Spirit.
>
> Romans 8:1

Hmm, that does not say there is some condemnation, or a little bit of condemnation, but *no* condemnation in Christ. None!

If there is no condemnation to those who are in Christ, and we are in Christ, then there is no condemnation toward us. The Lord surely is not putting condemnation on His children or speaking in a condemning tone, because that would be the Lord going against His Word and His nature. It would be unscriptural for Him to condemn us.

There is no condemnation in Christ.

Where the confusion comes from is in thinking that this Scripture is conditional; if we delve into the flesh, according to the second part of Romans 8:1, then God condemns. This belief is that if we stay in the Spirit, we are fine, but once we cross over into the flesh, then condemnation is God's correction and how He directs us to get us back on track. That is not accurate. God does not condemn us to show us the error of our ways. He does not have to, because the consequence of the sin does that automatically.

> For the wages of sin is death.
>
> Romans 6:23

When we are in the flesh, and when we sin, the result is always death. It is a natural consequence. We sin, and we reap the death it brings. So there *is* a condemnation of sorts: the consequences that sin brings, such as the negative outcomes in our lives and the heaviness and sorrow in our spirits. The consequences correct us. Our loving Father does not come over the top and heap condemnation on us when we are already hurting. Let me give you a tangible example that will help you see this more clearly.

As a parent, I tell my beautiful daughter not to come near the oven when I am about to open it. It is hot, and she can hurt herself. I do not tell her this because I am a dictator who wants to control her. I tell her this because I want to protect her. God's laws and ways are not to control us, but to lead us in the way we should go. They are instituted in order to bless and benefit us. If my daughter chooses to come touch the hot oven regardless of my instruction, then she reaps the result of that choice: she burns her fingers, it hurts and she cries. These are the consequences of her action. As her loving parent, I will not add to the pain of her natural consequences by saying, "Stupid! I told you so. You got what you deserved, because you didn't listen, dummy. I hope you're happy." That is condemnation, and that is the last thing I would say to my child, who I love so much. She touched the oven, experienced pain as a consequence, and that taught her all she needed to know.

As a loving parent, I say, "Oh honey, I know; I know it hurts. That's why I told you not to come close. Come here. Let me hold you. It's going to be okay. I'm here. I love you." And that is precisely how our loving heavenly parent, the Lord, deals with us after we fall short. When we make mistakes, He does not add condemnation on top of what we are already suffering. He gently and lovingly tends to our wounds and draws us unto Him through love until we get back on our feet and in the right space to carry on.

That is what it means to say, "There is no condemnation in Christ." God is not calling us names, pointing a finger or rubbing salt in the wound. He never corrects us, trains us or teaches us through condemnation.

All Scripture is given by inspiration of God, and is profitable for doctrine, for reproof, for correction, for instruction in righteousness.

2 Timothy 3:16

Just like the parent who gives his or her child instruction, God trains through instruction. Nevertheless, there is a condemning factor in the consequence of sin, but it is not coming from God—it comes from the sin itself. It is the natural reaction to the action. Mistaking guilt and condemnation for correction is a huge misconception among believers. Many Christians think feeling guilty is God correcting them. Nope, the difference between conviction and condemnation is in the *tone*. The enemy speaks through condemnation, but the Holy Spirit speaks through conviction.

Without proper discernment, we can mistake enemy persecution for God's correction. What usually happens is this: In the very moment the Holy Spirit quickens our spirit and we feel the gentle nudge of conviction, the enemy is lurking by the door to heap on a pile of condemning thoughts. We are bombarded with thoughts, such as *How could I have done that? I'm so stupid. Why do I keep making the same mistake over and over? How can I call myself a Christian? I'm such a hypocrite. Why can't I get it together?*

We hear thoughts like that, and we buy into them, believing they are valid, and even worse, believing they are from the Lord. Then, instead of being able to hear and receive clean correction through conviction, we fall into the pit of despair, spinning out about how bad we are, and how guilty we feel. We can stay in the condemnation pit for hours, days or even weeks. By the time we pull ourselves out, we barely remember what the Lord was trying to speak to us in the first place. The lesson gets lost and is not able to take root and elicit change. Can you see how drawing us into condemnation is a huge ploy of the enemy to keep us from moving forward?

Condemnation is an enemy tactic to prevent us from growing in the Lord.

The enemy uses thoughts and feelings of condemnation to distract us to the point where we are consumed with our failures, our mistakes and how bad we are. It is like a rattle with a baby. The enemy shakes the rattle and says, "Look over here. Look at your faults and how you've blown it. God is mad at you. You are a horrible Christian." Then we take our focus off the Lord and lose sight of what He was lovingly and gently pointing out to us, because He loves us and wants the best for us. That is how the enemy uses condemnation to derail us. He takes us around the same mountain of condemnation again and again, so we are never able to move forward. It is a big, painful distraction that is completely fruitless. It hurts our heart and our soul and does not benefit us one bit. Condemnation is a killer, and we do not have to go there. When we hear those thoughts or find ourselves sliding down that slippery slope, we can hold onto the truth of Scripture and pull ourselves the other way.

> There is therefore now no condemnation to those who are in Christ Jesus.
>
> Romans 8:1

Keep it simple: God good—enemy not good. God thoughts strengthen you, while enemy thoughts tear you down. God thoughts propel you forward, while enemy thoughts are a snare to halt your progress. Understanding the sound of the enemy and his tactics is the first step in avoiding the pitfalls he sets up in order to trap us.

11

Pitfalls

The greater the obstacle, the more
glory in overcoming it.

Moliere

Recognizing the Pitfalls

There are a handful of pitfalls that the enemy will attempt to lure you into while on-the-floor. With a newfound discernment between how God sounds and how the enemy sounds, you will be able to recognize those pitfalls as they unfold and have a greater capacity to resist them at the onset. You might still fall into a few. No big deal—just pull yourself out. No one is going to walk this Christian walk perfectly. It is not about being perfect; it is about the process. That is how we learn: We fall and get back up. When it comes to enemy tactics and pitfalls, the key is in seeing them. It is the *seeing* of them that enables you to avoid them. Once you know they are from the enemy, you are more able to identify and make choices.

The Pitfall of "This Is a Waste of Time"

You are on-the-floor, having set aside time to press into God, and are bombarded with thoughts like: *What am I doing, really? I'm just lying here. How is anything happening while I'm kind of doing nothing? Other people are out in the world making things happen. Is this just an excuse for me to do nothing? Am I being lazy? I'm not even really praying or reading the Word. How is lying here, quietly and still, doing anything? Am I wasting my time?*

Thoughts like this are a subtle form of warfare. The enemy is crafty; he knows that the most important thing we can do is lie at the feet of Jesus, and he will do anything he can to get us to do anything but that. He will make us think we are being lazy, so we will get up. He will fill our minds with things on our to-do list, and torment us that they are not getting done. He will taunt us with the thought that others are moving forward in life while we are losing ground.

Getting intimate, quiet and still with the Lord is posturing ourselves to connect with Him, hear Him and know Him. *Nothing* is more beneficial. *Nothing* will propel us into our destiny faster. It is common for us to spend much of our time on the go, but when we come out from among the harried pace of the world and separate ourselves unto God, only then can we truly find our lives and ourselves.

> For whoever desires to save his life will lose it, but whoever loses his life for My sake will find it.
>
> Matthew 16:25

We are not wasting time when we seek God first. When we do, He will make sure that everything we need is taken care of.

> Seek first the kingdom of God and His righteousness, and all these things shall be added to you.
>
> Matthew 6:33

That is quite a promise from God. If we seek Him first, He will take care of everything we need. No wonder the enemy lures us into constant busyness so that we are working harder and getting less in return. The enemy has us spinning and exhausted, running here and there, trying to "make our life happen," when God says our life is hidden in Him.

> For you died, and your life is hidden with Christ in God.
> Colossians 3:3

If we want to "find" our life, our destiny, our peace and our purpose, it is hidden in Him. As we seek Him and spend time with Him, our life is uncovered. It is so opposite of the worldly way of constant striving to get ahead. We are conditioned to expect accomplishment through constant action, but waiting on God is also a form of action. Sometimes being busy is not action at all. It is movement but not forward movement. Movement just for movement's sake is a setup.

The Pitfall of Busyness

Living in a constant state of busyness is more than having a type-A personality; it is more than being efficient or being a person who likes to get things accomplished. It is a trap, a pitfall and a tactic from the enemy to avoid feeling, dealing and healing. Think of B.U.S.Y. as being under Satan's yoke. Get still long enough and the Lord will show you what is behind the incessant activity. Then He will begin to heal you and grant you the capacity to be still. Remember, being still is where we begin to know Him and ourselves.

> Be still, and know that I am God.
> Psalm 46:10

To be still is some of the greatest "work" we can do in God. So, while you are on-the-floor seeking first His kingdom, and the enemy is doing everything he can to stop you, take this opportunity for the Lord to show you what is behind the busyness. Inquire of Him, "Lord, why am I always going, going, going? Why is it so challenging for me to be still?" As you ponder, the Holy Spirit might begin to take you back in time. Perhaps as a child you were rewarded for achievement. Maybe the only time a person in authority, like a parent or a teacher, expressed love to you was when you excelled. That could easily instill a pattern of association, such as "The more I do, the better I am." Therefore, who am I, and what good am I, if I am not producing? That is a life-changing understanding about yourself right there, and it could open the door to a huge internal shift. Major freedom can come from this kind of revelation as we begin to see that God values us for who we are, not what we do. As a result, much rest and peace are ushered in as the relentless drive for perfectionism is ushered out. Waiting on God is not a waste of time. It is time well spent that reaps tremendous rewards. A great man of prayer put it this way:

> It is a glorious thing to get to know God in a new way in the inner chamber. It is something still greater and more glorious to know God as the all-sufficient One, and to wait on His Spirit to open our hearts and minds wide to receive the great things, the new things, which He really longs to bestow on those who wait for Him.
>
> Andrew Murray

The Pitfall of Fear

Getting on-the-floor can be scary because you do not know what to expect. Purposely stepping into the unknown is not the easiest task. Most of us would rather not deal with our pain, so diving right into the middle of it might not be the most exciting idea at first. Fear of what may happen as you open yourself to emotions that have been under lock and key can be intense. You may have thoughts like, *Once I allow myself to tap in to those feelings, I won't be able to stop. They will overtake me. I'll have a breakdown and become a crazy person. I'll get hysterical and lose it. What's going to happen to me?*

You are not alone. It is absolutely normal to be wary and just plain scared. I assure you that I have yet to see anyone go off the deep end. I promise you this: You will *not* go crazy. The Lord will not allow that to happen. The Holy Spirit is gentle and will be with you the entire time. You can tread carefully and slowly. Go at your own pace. You do not need to uncover twenty years of issues in one session on-the-floor. Just allow the Lord to show you something and take you into it. He will be gentle and will never push you further than you want to go. The Lord is with you, but you are holding the reins; you are directing. When you say stop, you can stop. Recognize that fear is a tactic to keep you stagnant. See it for what it is and be willing to push through. That is faith. Faith is not stepping into what we see and know. Faith is taking a blind step, but knowing that the Lord will be there when we land and that we are safe.

> Faith is taking the first step even when you can't see the whole staircase.
>
> Martin Luther King Jr.

The Pitfall of Judgment and Condemnation

The enemy will throw darts of judgment and condemnation at you while you are on-the-floor, so knowing how to identify those thoughts, and recognizing they are not from God is crucial. As you begin to allow yourself to connect with your feelings, it can be tempting to judge them as petty. Thoughts like *It is so dumb that I'm upset over this. Other people have had it much worse. I'm making a big deal out of nothing.*

These types of thoughts might be stirring due to the fact that there was never a place made for your feelings growing up.

A family member, friend or parent might have said a similar version of the statements listed above to you, accused you of overreacting or insisted that you toughen up. Because of that, you learned early on to dismiss your emotions. On-the-floor is the time to get past that. Feelings are important, and yours matter. They might not have mattered to anyone in the past, but they matter to God, and you are not a big baby for having them. Make a decision to honor every emotion and every experience you have on-the-floor. Choose to believe they are worthy and valid. Others might not have made a place for your feelings in the past, and you might not have either, but you can now. It is a choice. Say out loud, "My feelings matter, and they are important to God."

God is not judging you, so you do not have to judge yourself either. For many of us, there is an inner struggle. On the outside we were doing a lot of things to get closer to God: going to church, reading the Bible and praying, but deep down we are actually scared to get too close to Him. We are pursuing Him, but on another level, either consciously or unconsciously, we are simultaneously keeping Him at arm's length. We think if we do hear His voice, all He is going to do is tell us how bad we are and point out all of our shortcomings. This is a big enemy lie. There is no need to fear God. *To fear Him*, according to Scripture, does not mean to be scared of Him. It means to be "in reverence, in wonder and in awe of Him—His greatness, and His majesty." He *is* awesome: awesome in His faithfulness to us, awesome in His unwavering love for us and awesome in His never-ending compassion for us. That is the true nature of God, and that is the God we will meet as we pursue Him. Remember, there is no condemnation to those who are in Christ (see Romans 8:1).

Accepting and receiving ourselves can be just as difficult as believing that the Lord accepts and receives us, and it will take practice for those to whom it does not come naturally. If this is especially difficult for you, imagine how you would be with your child or someone else you love dearly. You would not call his or her feelings stupid. Apply the same grace and compassion for yourself that you would for someone else. You are worth the same amount of acceptance.

Judgment and condemnation are from the enemy and are used to block us from going deeper. They are a ploy to turn us against ourselves and distract us from the real issue. It takes discernment to distinguish between God's voice and the enemy's voice and lots and lots of practice to be able to self-examine without judgment or condemnation, especially when more intense issues rise to the surface. Maybe you have lied, cheated, committed adultery or had an abortion. Deep feelings of shame might surface as you revisit some of these experiences. Shame is not from God, and He is not judging you about anything. Not one thing. We have all made mistakes and wrong choices. The enemy likes to remind us of our past mistakes. He brings them up again and again and again to torment us. When we go to the Lord and ask for forgiveness, He wipes the slate clean—completely clean. It is literally like it never happened in God's eyes. You don't have to repent for the same thing over and over. The Lord will not continue to bring up your past, and you do not have to either.

> For as the heavens are high above the earth, so great is His mercy toward those who fear Him; as far as the east is from the west, so far has He removed our transgressions from us.
>
> Psalm 103:11–12

He removes our transgressions and takes our sin and our mistakes as far as the east is from the west. He is not holding anything over our heads. If God is not holding anything against you, why are you continuing to hold things against yourself?

He has forgiven you, and you can forgive you, too. The Lord does not remind us of how bad we were, or of the mistakes we have made. He restores us back to wholeness and purity, regardless of what happened in our past.

God is a restorer, not a reminder.

God is never harsh or critical. That is not His nature. If you hear things, such as "You got what you deserved because you were disobedient" or "It is your own fault that happened to you," those thoughts are not from God. If you feel worthless, tarnished or like used goods, those are precisely the areas in which the Lord can bring healing. You might feel the way you do about yourself because of the extreme circumstances you have endured, but that is not what is true about you. What is true is this: You are holy and blameless in God's sight (see Colossians 1:22).

The Pitfall of Confusion

When you are on-the-floor asking the Holy Spirit to reveal something to you, He will. What you receive from Him is often the first thought, unction or picture that comes to mind. Invariably, your very next thought will be, *Is this really God speaking to me, or am I just making it up? When I hear nice things about myself, is that the Lord talking, or is it my wishful thinking?* Thoughts like these *will* arise in an attempt to get you spinning and questioning. Expect them, and stop them at their onset. Once you have done that, trust what you are sensing and hearing, as well as the pictures that are being revealed to you as you wait on the Holy Spirit.

The bottom line is trust yourself. The Lord often speaks through our very first unction or thought, but we assume it cannot be that easy. Then fear comes in and we start second-guessing. Do not second-guess while on-the-floor. The Holy Spirit is with you. Choose to believe that what you are hearing and what you are sensing in your spirit is right and good. You may ask, "But how can I be sure?" Knowing if what you are hearing is from God or from your own soul—your mind, will and emotions—is not as crucial in this situation. Differentiating between God and the enemy is foremost, and one way to do that is to tune in to the tone and spirit behind what you are hearing. If what you are sensing is coming from your soul and not God's Spirit, but it is uplifting and aligns with God's Word, then it is still beneficial. What comes from the enemy is never beneficial. If it is critical, harsh or judgmental, then throw it out. As long as what you are hearing is not condemning, whether it is from God's Spirit or your own, it is of value when on-the-floor. Go with it. Go with that first thing that pops up. Make a decision to trust it. Trust God and trust yourself.

When it comes to trusting the first thing you hear keep in mind the context to which I am referring: on-the-floor time, when you are seeking insight into who you are, what you have been through and why you think, feel and react the way you do. However, when making big life decisions always use wisdom and proceed with care. In the case of a major decision, I would not recommend acting hastily, but encourage you to continue earnestly in prayer over time until the Lord confirms what you are sensing. I have found that when something is from God, He will say it more than once. And when making an important decision it can also be wise to adhere to this Scripture:

In a multitude of counselors there is safety.

Proverbs 24:6

So, our goal is to trust but also to use wisdom, especially when it comes to making decisions based on what we sense in prayer.

Some of the most freeing words the Lord has ever spoken to me were on this very topic. I was so hesitant to make any decision because I was fearful I was not hearing God and that I would move out of His will. One day He spoke to me in my spirit and said, "Just step out. Make a decision. You do not have to worry. All you have to do is stay close to Me. If you misstep, I will course correct you, but I cannot course correct you if you do not move." Later I came across this quote that confirmed what the Lord had stated:

You cannot guide a ship that's parked.

Myles Munroe

So my job was to hear Him as best I could, be willing to step out in faith and, above all else, stay close to Him. If I made a wrong step, it would not be the end of the world. The Lord promised that He would let me know. The paralyzing fear of "getting it wrong" keeps us stagnant and is another enemy tactic. Push against timidity, and go for it. If you make a mistake, but stay close to the Lord, He will get you back on track.

The Pitfall of Anger toward God

Thoughts and feelings toward God might begin to surface like: *Where were You, God, when I went through this? Why did You allow all these things to happen to me? I don't feel safe with You. I know I'm supposed to love You and trust You, but I feel betrayed and confused and angry with You. Why didn't You protect me?*

Reconnecting with wounds from your past might bring up negative feelings toward God. It is difficult for many of us to open ourselves up to God at all because deep down we do not trust Him. How can we go to God for healing when, in our heart of hearts, we feel like He abandoned us?

It is not easy to face that you might be angry with God. You are not alone in this, and you do not have to feel guilty about it either. Being mad at Him can be a tough one because as Christians, the last thing we want to admit is that we are resentful toward God. On top of being angry with Him, we then feel condemned for feeling angry with Him. You confess to harboring resentment, and *wham*, condemnation from the enemy is waiting at the door to barrage you. It is the one-two punch. The enemy is the one who harms us, but he fools us into thinking *God* is the one who hurts us, so that we get mad at God. Then, when we are trying to process our anger, the enemy comes in to make us feel guilty for being mad at God. What a setup!

One of the number one tactics of the enemy is getting us to blame God for what the enemy has done.

Unless we have extreme discernment and understanding of the enemy, it is easy to fall into the trap of blaming God. One of the enemy's greatest ploys is to get us to blame God for something God did not do. This can happen when someone we love dies, for example. Without proper understanding the first thought might be, *Why did God take them?* Well-meaning but uninformed Christians reinforce this wrong belief by saying something along the lines of "God needed them in heaven," which can be even more difficult to process. Then you are left with, *Why would God take away someone I love? Why did God do this to me?*

It is in these types of sensitive situations that, because of lack of knowledge, false doctrines and beliefs are formed.

My people are destroyed for lack of knowledge.

Hosea 4:6

Believing God killed someone you love is a lack of understanding. God does not kill people so they can be with Him in heaven. He does not withhold or steal or kill. That is the enemy's job. God is a giver of life. True doctrine is that Jesus gives life, and the enemy steals life.

> The thief does not come except to steal, and to kill, and to destroy. I have come that they may have life, and that they may have it more abundantly.
>
> John 10:10

The grief of losing someone we love can be so extreme that we do not know how to get through it. Believing that God is to blame adds to the grief and throws us into confusion. Are we not supposed to trust God, and believe that He is good?

We need God's comfort most during a traumatic experience, but how can we turn to Him when we think that He is the cause of our excruciating pain? We must see this for what it is: a crafty move on the enemy's part. He wants to turn us against the Lord when we need Him the most. He would like nothing more than to coax us into harboring resentment toward the One who promises comfort in our time of need.

Feeling betrayed by God produces a deep wound. Learning the truth that He is not the one inflicting loss and pain does not mean that those negative feelings evaporate instantly. There still could be unanswered questions and a lot of whys stirring in your heart. Guess what? God does not get mad at us for being mad at Him. He knows that we have been duped by the enemy into believing that He is the one who hurt us. The Lord knows all. He is omniscient, remember? He knows everything, and He loves us regardless, and He knows the tactics of the enemy better than anyone.

It is okay if we are mad at God, but we don't want to stay that way because harboring resentment and being angry with God stalls our healing. Shift the blame onto the true culprit so that your heart will be open to receive the love that God has for you. These are areas and issues to work through slowly and gently with the Lord. Believing that God is good is a start. It might take some time for that understanding to go from your head to your heart. Work through it, and walk through it with Him. Some of your on-the-floor time might best be spent dealing with how you feel about the Lord. There is no sense in going to the Lord and pretending everything is okay—especially in regard to your feelings about Him. Just lay everything out there and be real. He already knows. You are not hiding anything from Him. Admit resentment or anger to yourself and to Him, and allow Him to bring you through it.

The Pitfall of Self-Pity

Self-pity is our worst enemy.

Helen Keller

Watch out! Self-pity is deep and the slope is slippery; this might be the biggest and baddest pitfall of all. It is definitely the sneakiest, and once you fall in, it is not so easy to get out. There exists a fine line between grieving and sliding into self-pity. A truly healing cry has a certain feel to it. It feels . . . clean. Self-pity has a different feel and a different tone—the why-me-poor-me tone. How do we navigate the difference between healing, grieving and self-pity? Here is the deal: Only you can discern it for yourself. You have to learn to sense the difference. When you feel yourself crossing over into the poor-me zone, you need to recognize it, and pull yourself in the other direction. Permitting and wallowing in self-pity interrupts the healing process.

I had a revelatory moment on-the-floor regarding this very subject. I was in the middle of some deep feelings when self-pity started creeping in. I found myself starting to go into the whys: *Why didn't I have parents who were there for me? Why have I been so alone? Why did all this happen to me? When I look at other people's lives they seem to have it so easy. It's not fair. Why me?* The Holy Spirit came in powerfully in that moment and flooded me with understanding. He revealed to me that the Lord knew exactly what He was doing. Even though it grieved Him to see me grieve and have to go through painful experiences, He knitted all the components of my life's experiences together according to me and my destiny.

He showed me that had I come from a more secure family, I most likely would not have had the same fervency for Him. Because my parents were disconnected from each other and from me, my desperation for intimacy and connection drove me to God. Because of what I went through and according to how He made me, I was impelled to go into deep places with the Lord where many would not go. I *had* to go to those places. I needed God's presence like I needed water, and not only for myself, but in time, I would assist others by teaching them how to go there as well. With this revelation, I was able to see my tribulation from a different perspective. I was no longer enveloped with the self-pitying, enemy-induced thoughts of *Why did I have to go through this?* Instead I actually saw what I had experienced as a blessing and a Holy Spirit setup. This revelation lined up with how God orchestrated my calling, destiny and purpose, and it is what constructed the foundation and the fabric of my ministry. That understanding caused me to look at what I had endured in an entirely different way. It shed a new light and helped me avoid the trap of self-pity the next time I felt it creeping in.

God does not inflict painful situations upon us to teach us lessons. That is more false doctrine. Remember, God—good, enemy—bad. But if we allow Him, God *will* use what the enemy had planned to destroy us for His good, for a greater purpose and to build and strengthen us.

> And we know that all things work together for good to those who love God, to those who are the called according to His purpose. For whom He foreknew, He also predestined to be conformed to the image of His Son, that He might be the first-born among many brethren. Moreover whom He predestined, these He also called; whom He called, these He also justified; and whom He justified, these He also glorified. What then shall we say to these things? If God is for us, who can be against us?
>
> Romans 8:28–31

Do not buy into the lie that God put you in an abusive situation because it was a part of your destiny. No, God does not orchestrate harmful situations for life lessons, but He *will* use every hurtful, damaging thing that the enemy has afflicted upon us for our greater good. As the verse above says, if God is for us, who or what can successfully prevail against us? Nothing and no thing! So, when you are on-the-floor, be aware. If you find yourself sliding into self-pity, do everything in your power to pull yourself the other way. If the lure to fall into self-pity is too strong, then get up if need be and say, "Lord, I'm going to revisit this area later." Then go do something light and easy that you enjoy and just chill out. There is no pressure. Remember that the whys can trigger self-pity. If you have a question, ask the Lord for understanding, but do not allow yourself to go into the why-me place of despair.

The Pitfall of Despair

Grief, like self-pity, is tricky. It can be like quicksand that grabs ahold of you, and before you know it, you are completely submerged and suffocating. How do we allow ourselves to feel grief and move through it without getting stuck in the pit of ongoing despair? This is another fine line that must be walked carefully. When it comes to these heavy-duty situations, we must be on the lookout: keen, alert and aware of the traps as we navigate through them. We want to allow ourselves to go into the pain but make sure we come out the other side healthy and whole. Think of it like climbers and campers. Climbers explore the terrain; they go through and keep on moving, but campers pitch a tent and settle in for a while. Grief is an emotion to visit, explore and move through, but you do not want to live there. Feel it, but keep in mind that you want to move through it, not set up camp. Be aware of the thoughts that attempt to suck you into lasting despair. If you find yourself settling in, use your will and shift yourself out to the best of your ability.

The Pitfall of Nothing Happened

You are on-the-floor trying to connect, trying to go deep, trying to explore and . . . nothing. You feel absolutely nothing, not a thing. This is actually a pitfall, too, and brings with it thoughts, such as *Nothing is happening, what's wrong with me? I must not be doing it right.* (Condemnation alert!) *What is wrong with God, and why isn't He walking me through this?* (Judgment alert!)

There is *nothing* wrong with you or with God. I did not have a powerful experience every single time I was on-the-floor and you probably will not either. You may have many on-the-floor times where you do not experience much of anything at all. Do not allow yourself to get frustrated. Our relationship with God is just that, a relationship, and like all relationships, there is an ebb and flow. Sometimes you connect, and sometimes you do not. Sometimes you feel close, and sometimes you do not. No need to overanalyze. If nothing happens on-the-floor, shake it off and go about your day. Do not strive over it. God is not going anywhere and neither is the floor. You can revisit both later.

Entering into God's presence and connecting with Him is learned behavior. God is always with us, but often it takes time for us to learn how to connect and enter in. When we do this, we are practicing—practicing the presence of God. Soon you *will* have an experience with Him, and when you do, you will be grateful for all the time you devoted to pursuing Him. Finding God is worth every minute invested.

> Then you will call upon Me and go and pray to Me, and I will listen to you. And you will seek Me and find Me, when you search for Me with all your heart.
>
> Jeremiah 29:12–13

There is no formula for how to do this the "right" way. Some may have an immediate experience. For others it may take a week, a few months or maybe even longer. Keep in mind that many of us are so wounded, shut down and disconnected emotionally that opening up might take time—a lot of time. There might be so much fear present, that on some level, you resist and put up a block, even if you are not aware that you are doing so. Or you may believe that you have no emotions to explore. Ha! If you are breathing, you have feelings to explore, but you might be so used to trivializing your pain that you do not think you have any. Be patient with yourself, and make a commitment to just do it. If you set aside the time to meet God, He will meet you there. If you are hungry for God, and desperate for Him, you will find Him. Scripture teaches us that if we give God our time, we will be rewarded.

> Ask, and it will be given to you; seek, and you will find; knock, and it will be opened to you. For everyone who asks receives, and he who seeks finds, and to him who knocks it will be opened.
>
> Matthew 7:7–8

Think of "ask" as an acronym that stands for **A**sk, **S**eek, and **K**nock. It is our job to ask, seek and knock, and it is His job to answer. I guarantee you, literally guarantee you, that if you are persistent, something, at some time, *will* happen. Be committed to building a habit of on-the-floor time regardless of what you experience. Be tenacious. Make a decision to sow the time. God promises that if you make a habit of giving Him a portion of your time and pouring out your heart to Him, He will meet you there.

> I love those who love me, and those who seek me diligently will find me.

> Proverbs 8:17

Develop this mindset: "God, your Word says that if I ask, seek and knock I will find You. I expect that to happen, and I'm going to keep at it for as long as it takes." Now, that is a powerful mindset.

> Patience and diligence, like faith, remove mountains.

> William Penn

Time on-the-floor is not about trying to change yourself or about stopping counterfeit comfort behavior. It is about connecting. The behavior will change in time and will become a product of your intimacy with Him. This does not happen overnight. Few milestones are achieved overnight—but through patience, perseverance and a little something called . . . process.

12

The Purpose of Process

It is good to have an end to journey toward;
but it is the journey that matters, in the end.

Ernest Hemingway

The Benefits of Process

Process is not always our favorite experience. It means waiting, and we are a people that does not like to wait. We like things fast; we want it now. Actually, we wanted it yesterday. There is a season for everything—a time to plant and a time to reap. The principle behind how things unfold during seasons can be found in both the Bible and in the natural realm. It is called seedtime and harvest. We plant a seed, we wait, and, in time, we can expect a harvest from that seed. What is in between seedtime and reaping a harvest is inherent in the name itself: *time*. The order is seed, then *time*, and then harvest. We do not plant a seed and see a harvest that day, or the next day or the next. There is always a waiting period, and the wait time can feel long. It may be seed, time and harvest, but it can feel more like seed, tiiiiiiiiiiiiiiiiiiiiiiiiiiime and harvest. If we had things our way, we would plant a seed and have a mature tree in five minutes, but that is not how things work. The Lord can and will perform miracles where no waiting is involved, but we will always have at least one area, probably a lot more than one, where we have to walk something out and endure process. Why? What is the point in all this waiting? Obviously, there must be a reason if God designed it this way, so what is it?

Process Produces Character

But we also glory in tribulations, knowing that tribulation produces perseverance; and perseverance, character; and character, hope.

Romans 5:3–4

A Scripture like that can stir up some emotions. While we are waiting, we are not always so interested in perseverance and character. We become tired of waiting and ready for the promise to get here already, but waiting develops qualities that cannot be gleaned any other way. Just like a seed takes time to develop and mature, so do we. As we wait and endure, character is being produced in us.

Character cannot be developed in ease and quiet. Only through experience of trial and suffering can the soul be strengthened, ambition inspired, and success achieved.

Helen Keller

Our heavenly Father is not keeping blessings from us to teach us a lesson. He is not holding back because He is mean and does not want to give to us. God is not a withholder; that is not His nature. It is His good pleasure to see us prosper and be blessed.

> Let them shout for joy and be glad, who favor my righteous cause; and let them say continually, "Let the LORD be magnified, who has pleasure in the prosperity of His servant."
>
> Psalm 35:27

He loves us so much that He does not want to promote us until we are equipped and mature enough to handle it. Our earthly father did not give us keys and access to the family car when we were ten years old. First of all, that would have been illegal, but also, we were not mature or skilled enough at that age to handle the responsibility. We were not ready for it. As much as our earthly father and heavenly Father want to bless us, they know that a blessing given before we are ready can actually harm us more than help us.

We can be like spoiled children. We want stuff when we want it and are not always able to recognize what is required character-wise to handle everything God has for us. Our heavenly Father is conditioning us to not only receive our blessings, but to be able to hold onto them. He is waiting until we have strengthened and matured, knowing that a promise gained too soon can bring destruction.

Process Prepares and Protects

You might think, *I just want to be married.* Try being married without character traits like patience and longsuffering being developed and see how far that takes you. Or you imagine, *I just want to be successful.* Acquire money without maturity and foundation in yourself and in the Lord, and see how quickly the blessing of finances can destroy you. Or you dream, *I just want to be a star.* Try standing up under the pressures of fame without having the strength built inside of yourself to resist temptation and compromise and see how quickly the very fame and finances you prayed for will be instrumental in your demise.

Gifts are great and blessings are wonderful, but without preparation and maturity a blessing can quickly become a curse. Character is the foundation our gift must rest upon, or our gift can wind up hurting us. You do not want your gift to take you where your character cannot keep you.

We must be prepared in order to be preserved and not destroyed. It is the inner work that prepares us to receive and hold onto the outer blessings. Waiting is an inner work used to temper and strengthen us to be able to manage all the Father has for us. It is easy for the Lord to bring us stuff: a spouse, a car or a home. It is the work He does within us that is more challenging. Much of our walk with the Lord is about the inner work. He often uses our circumstances—what is or is not happening on the outside—to perfect our insides. Enduring these trials is what builds character and teaches us what it means to live by faith.

Process Cultivates Faith

Waiting trains us to walk by faith. Faith is more than something we say; it is a position we live within. True faith is a place of belief and knowing that does not happen overnight. It is produced by holding fast to what we believe even when what we see and what we feel is contrary.

For we walk by faith, not by sight.

2 Corinthians 5:7

This is the essence of faith; believing what you cannot yet see. If you can see it, it is not faith.

Faith is the substance of things hoped for, the evidence of things not seen.

Hebrews 11:1

We have to do our believing before we obtain the promise. The process challenges us, but that is the way the Kingdom works. We are constantly challenged in our choices. Will we stay the course until the answer comes, or veer off the path prior to the promise being fulfilled? There is a purpose to the waiting process. It teaches us true dependence on the Lord, and what it is to really trust in Him. This is the kind of faith that stands strong in adversity.

Process Reveals

Adverse circumstances reveal what we really believe. It is easy to have faith when all is well, but when things get difficult and our back is up against the wall, we see just how strong our faith truly is.

If you faint in the day of adversity, your strength is small.

Proverbs 24:10

Faith without sight, in the midst of adversity, is the result of a deeper work that manifests when we stand through trials and choose to believe regardless of our circumstances. Smith Wigglesworth, a man of great faith said, "I'm not moved by what I see. I'm not moved by what I feel. I'm only moved by what I believe." I bet he was not born with that resolve, but came into that unwavering position through a lot of waiting, learning, growing, failing, falling and getting back up. In other words, process.

Process Shapes Belief

There is something about enduring process that transfers knowledge past our heads and into our hearts so that we know it, we get it, we live it and breathe it. That is revelation knowledge, the place where we know that we know, and revelation, once garnered, is not easily lost. Without true revelation, it is easy to forget.

> But be doers of the word, and not hearers only, deceiving yourselves. For if anyone is a hearer of the word and not a doer, he is like a man observing his natural face in a mirror; for he observes himself, goes away, and immediately forgets what kind of man he was.
>
> James 1:22–24

We look in the mirror and see clearly, but when we turn away we quickly forget who we are. That happens because the truth has not taken root. We learn an idea, but it is not deep enough in our spirit and belief system yet. We hear truth and receive it, but an hour later it can be like we never heard it at all, as if we are programmed to forget. That is why it takes time, practice, repetition and experience to establish the truth into us so that it becomes weaved into the fabric of who we are.

Process Strengthens

In chapter fifteen of the gospel of John, Jesus refers to Himself as the vine, the Father is the vinedresser, and we are the branches. There are a number of metaphors in the Word that use grapes and vines. Knowing that the Lord does not do anything by happenstance, I did a little study on vine dressing. I wondered if there was a correlation between how grapes are grown and how God grows us, and of course, there is one.

There are a couple of key factors in producing high-quality grapes that in turn make for an excellent wine. The grapes must be grown in adverse circumstances. The vines must be planted closely together and with their water supply severely restricted. If you take a grapevine and make its growing environment too comfortable and its water and nutrients easily accessible, it will give you poor grapes. This is because the grapevine has a choice. Given a favorable environment, it will choose to take the vegetative route. This means it will put its energies into making leaves and shoots. In a way, it is saying, "This is a nice, comfortable spot; I'm going to make myself at home here." Therefore, the plant will not be too bothered with making grapes. But make things difficult for the vine by restricting water supply, making nutrients scarce, pruning it hard and crowding it with close neighbors, and it will sense that this is not the ideal place to be a grapevine. Instead of devoting itself to growing big and sprawling, it will focus its effort on reproducing itself, which for a vine means making grapes.

Grapevines are a lot like people. Place someone in a near-perfect environment, giving them every comfort and all that they could ever want to satisfy their needs, and you could have disastrous consequences. Adverse conditions produce a better grape and a better us. When we are getting squeezed, it is for a purpose.

> For I know the thoughts that I think toward you, says the LORD, thoughts of peace and not of evil, to give you a future and a hope.
>
> Jeremiah 29:11

God knows what He is doing, and it is not to harm us, but to prepare us to be all that we can be.

Process Produces Fruit

Along the road of process we have choices. It is up to us whether we allow the adverse circumstances to steal our hope or allow them to strengthen our resolve. It is all about choice and perspective. A long and arduous process produces one of two fruits: doubt or faith. We can question God—and allow frustration and despair to set in—or hold fast to our faith and persevere. This is what Paul says about Abraham:

> He did not waver at the promise of God through unbelief, but was strengthened in faith, giving glory to God, and being fully convinced that what He had promised He was also able to perform.
>
> Romans 4:20–21

Abraham kept his eyes on the promise, not on the circumstances. He was certain God could and would come through for him. We should want to develop the same resolve. When in doubt, shift yourself out. Shift yourself out of the fear, questioning and result-oriented thinking, and into trusting God and the process. Choose faith. Love believes the best in all situations (see 1 Corinthians 13:7), so in order for us to walk in love, we must choose to believe the best about God's intent for us. The best means *knowing* that all things work together for our good (see Romans 8:28), and that there is purpose to our process.

Process might appear to be halting our progress, but in truth, it is preparing us for our destiny. In the end, it is not how quickly we are moving, but what is happening within us *as* we are moving. Above all, it is most important that we continue moving. We must keep on keeping on, full of faith and trusting God, with our eye on the prize.

I am a slow walker, but I never walk back.

Abraham Lincoln

13

Potholes to Process

Hold the vision. Trust the process.

Unknown

Recognizing the Potholes

Just as there are pitfalls while on-the-floor, there are a few potholes that we can accidentally fall into along the road of process, hazards that are strategically laid by the enemy to get us discouraged and off track. If we know what they are in advance, we can move through our healing with greater ease.

POTHOLE—Evaluating Progress during Process

Evaluating your progress by what you see and what you feel will not give you an accurate assessment of your growth. When change does not happen as quickly as we would like, we often wonder if it is happening at all. Growth is not always easy to see, and we cannot rely on our natural senses to estimate our progression.

When a woman is pregnant, she may not look or feel pregnant for months. To the naked eye, it may appear that nothing is happening, yet every day numerous things are changing and growing and being formed in the most intricate of ways inside of her. The same is true when it comes to measuring our growth, so do not be fooled. Just because you do not see or feel change, that does not mean change is not occurring.

God's work in us is not futile. More is happening than you know. Trust that work, and in time you will see it. Just like the pregnant woman who shows no obvious evidence of pregnancy, and then—pop!—everything that has been growing inside of her begins to show, in due season, everything that God is forming on the inside of you will become evident as well.

POTHOLE—God, Where Are You?

Process can be a lonely time, and it can feel like God is not helping. Why does the Lord, who loves us, allow us to go through such difficulty when He could easily extend a hand and make things much easier? It reminds me of the story of the boy and the butterfly.

One day a little boy was playing outdoors and stumbled upon a caterpillar. Carefully, he picked it up and took it home to show his mother. He asked his mother if he could keep it, and she said he could if he would take good care of it. The boy found a large jar and put inside it plants to eat and a stick for the caterpillar to climb. Every day he watched the caterpillar and brought it new plants to eat. One day, the caterpillar climbed up the stick and started acting strangely. The boy called his mom, who explained that the caterpillar was building a cocoon. It would spend time in the cocoon and then transform into a butterfly.

The boy watched every day, waiting for the butterfly to emerge. Then one day it happened, a small hole appeared in the cocoon and the butterfly started to struggle to come out. At first the boy was excited, but soon he became troubled. The butterfly was struggling so hard. It did not seem like it was making any progress and looked like it was not going to be able to get out and break free. The boy was so concerned that he decided to help. He ran to get scissors. Then he snipped the cocoon to make the hole bigger, and the butterfly quickly emerged. As the butterfly came out the boy was surprised. It did not look right. It had a swollen body and small, shriveled wings. He continued to watch the butterfly, expecting that at any moment the wings would dry out, enlarge and expand to support the swollen body. But that did not happen.

He went online and researched the metamorphosis of a butterfly and learned that the butterfly is supposed to struggle. In fact, the butterfly's struggle to push its way through the tiny opening of the cocoon forces the fluid out of its body and into its wings. Without the struggle, the butterfly would never fly. Even though the boy's intentions were good, his act of compassion hurt the butterfly. The butterfly spent the rest of its life crawling around with a swollen body and shriveled wings never able to fly.

Sometimes we are tempted to fall into the trap of resenting God with thoughts, such as *Why aren't You helping me? Why are You letting me go through this, God? Why don't You love me? If You loved me You would make it all stop.* When these thoughts come, remember the butterfly. The Lord does love us, which is why He does not just come in and snip the cocoon open for us. He wants us to fly, He built us to fly and He knows what we need in order to reach our capabilities. Just as the butterfly is developed through adversity, so are we. It might seem like

God is not compassionate, but He knows what He is doing in allowing us to endure. There is a purpose in the process.

The struggle you're in today is developing the strength you need for tomorrow.

Robert Tew

POTHOLE—Fatigue and Frustration

After a long season of waiting, your heart's cry might become, *How much longer, Lord? How much longer do I have to endure this? I can't take it anymore!* This is another mindset and enemy snare. Do not fall into the trap and buy into this type of thinking. The enemy will attempt to lure us into fatigue and frustration because time is passing by, and we do not know how long we will be in this place. We must resist him and hold fast to the Word of God. Here are two Scriptures to stand on:

I can do all things through Christ who strengthens me.

Philippians 4:13

Trust in the LORD with all your heart, and lean not on your own understanding; in all your ways acknowledge Him, and He shall direct your paths.

Proverbs 3:5–6

At times, it might feel like what we are going through is more than we can bear, but the good news is you will not be in this tough spot forever. You will get through; it is only temporary.

Transition is a state that literally means "an in-between place." It is not a place to settle. It is not a place to inhabit. It is an interim place, a place to move through. You will get through to the other side, and you do not have to do anything to make it happen faster. In fact, often you cannot do anything to make it happen faster or move the process along. You have to be still and allow it to unfold. Just as children cannot will themselves older no matter how hard they try, we cannot muscle our way through process to expedite the situation—no matter how many books we read or Bible studies we attend.

We rest in Him, and the rest is up to Him.

There are ordained times and seasons of rest. We rest while the Lord is restoring us. Notice that the root word of restoration is *rest*. It is not called *work*storation or *try*storation or *strive*storation, but *rest*oration. Our "work" during these times is to stay in faith and trust that when God is involved, things are happening. We can choose to be at peace, believing and expecting that all will unfold in God's ordained and perfect timing. Not what we think is perfect timing, but God's perfect timing. He is the Potter, and we are the clay. The clay does not form itself, and neither do we. Our job is to stay malleable so that He can mold and shape us. We stay malleable by staying in His presence. The rest is up to Him.

Embracing Process

"Okay, hold on here," you might say. "I not only have to accept process, but now I'm supposed to like it?" Well, you don't have to, but there is great value in learning not only to accept process, but to actually enjoy it. We spend the majority of our lives in the midst of process, so if we want to be happy for the majority of our lives, then we had better learn to enjoy process. To only be happy during select moments of achievement means that we are only going to be happy during a handful of moments. I do not want to be happy for 5 percent of my life, so I choose to be happy now and find joy in the moments of great achievement, as well as joy along the long road to reaching said achievement.

Process is not what happens on our way to life. Process *is* our life. We can easily reside within a mindset of perpetual striving. It is the I-will-be-happy-when syndrome. It goes something like this: I will be happy when I get married, when I lose ten pounds, get the promotion or buy the house. It is almost as if we put off enjoying life until we get "there." The only problem is, that dang *there* keeps moving. As soon as you get *it* or get *there*, another *it* and a new *there* come along. When our happiness is tied to a future goal or event, it is a setup to keep us striving toward a dangling carrot that is perpetually outside of our grasp. We never catch it; therefore, we are never fully happy. I choose to be happy now, be happy along the way and be happy when I get *there*. This ups my happiness percentage from 5 percent of the time to more like 95 percent of the time—a much better way to live.

Does this mean that we should be content with what we have and where we are and not set goals or dream for greater? No, I am not saying that, not even close; but I refuse to be happy only when I get *there*, because I am wise enough to know that there is no *there*, only *here*. And if I am not happy *here*, then I won't be happy when I get *there* either. Loving process does not come naturally. It is a choice, it is a shift in mindset and it is a learned love.

Develop a Love-to-Learn Attitude

I love to learn. At ninety years old, I will be investing in my growth. I will be discovering new things about myself, about the Lord, about my husband and children and about life. I plan on trying things I have never tried, taking interesting classes and exploring new lands. I choose to love to learn and plan on continuing to learn and grow until my last day on earth. That is what makes life exciting. Knowing everything does not make life exciting. Change might be scary, but it is also stimulating. Too much sameness is boring and monotonous. Life is meant to keep moving, growing and evolving. We cannot become like stagnant water. In order to stay fresh, we must continue flowing and growing.

Process is inevitable—there is no way around it—but our experience during process is up to us. We can be full of anticipation and excited about the unknown and what is to come, or we can be in a constant state of fretfulness and put our joy off until later. I choose the former, and you have a choice, too. Ask yourself: "What am I waiting for to be happy? Can I shift my perspective and choose to be happy now?"

Life is a journey, not a destination.

Ralph Waldo Emerson

14

Out with the Old and In with the New

If anyone is in Christ, he is a new creation;
old things have passed away;
behold, all things have become new.

2 Corinthians 5:17

The Stages

When we accept Christ we become spiritually new in an instant, but it takes time for the rest of us to catch up. Becoming mentally new and emotionally new happens in stages. Because these stages are internal, and not always tangible, it can be challenging to discern where you are and what is happening. This process is individual and personal, so there is no formula, but as you come out of the old and into the new, there are some common stops along the way. As you enter and move through these stages, let them serve as lampposts to you, so you know that something real is happening; you are not crazy, and you are, actually, right on track.

Stage One—Letting Go

Coming into the new cannot happen until we willingly decide to let go of the old. Our Lord is changing our insides, and we need to create a space for the new to be received.

> And no one puts new wine into old wineskins; or else the new wine bursts the wineskins, the wine is spilled, and the wineskins are ruined. But new wine must be put into new wineskins.
>
> Mark 2:22–23

He is shaping each one of us into a new vessel to carry a new thing. That means emptying out the old in order to be filled with the new. We do that by letting go. This is the thing with letting go: It is simple, but not easy. It can be easier to hold onto the counterfeit than to have to experience the hole in our soul. It can be easier to stay in the wrong relationship than to have no relationship. It can be easier to take the recreational drug than to have to feel the shame it is masking. Sometimes it is more comforting to have the wrong something than nothing at all. Having nothing is an uncomfortable place to be. Empty is challenging. Leaving what we have become accustomed to and what is familiar is not easy. We are usually willing to let go of the old once what is new is firmly in our sights, or better yet, in our grasp. However, with the Lord, it rarely works that way. He likes us to step out into the unknown and trust Him. After we take the step of faith, He will usher in the new.

> Faith is a process of leaping into the abyss not on the basis of any certainty about where we shall land, but rather on the belief that we shall land.
>
> Carter Heyward

Stage Two—Grieving

As old junk is broken off, we begin to go through a type of grieving process. This can mean letting go of counterfeit comforts, relationships or old thought patterns. The letting go of anything familiar can trigger grief. Even though what we are letting go of and what is being loosed is something we desperately want gone, it has been with us for so long that it has become a part of who we are. In some ways, it has shaped our identity, so being without it feels strange, foreign and extremely uncomfortable. You may not be able to put your finger on it, but you know something is missing, and its absence brings up sadness, an eerie sorrow. It helps to understand that this is a completely natural and normal part of the process. A death has occurred. A death of something we want dead, but a death nonetheless. And when something dies, when a part of us no longer exists, we grieve the loss of it.

You might be wondering how you can let go of a counterfeit comfort when it might be one of the few places you find solace. How do you intentionally release perhaps the only thing in life from where you derive pleasure, even if the pleasure is fleeting? I know—that is a hard one. I felt that way about cigarettes. They enslaved me; I hated them, but at the same time they were like best friends. They were my constant companions as I moved through my day. Cigarettes were by my side at the end of every meal and the start of every phone conversation. We hung out with each other before bed and woke to greet the day with one another each morning. Cigarettes shared in my celebrations and my disappointments, and above all else, they were always there for me when I needed them. It is not easy letting go of something so close to us, even if that something is killing us. And when we do, there will most likely be a bit of grieving. Something that was a part of you is gone, and you find yourself in a strange, unfamiliar, uncomfortable place where the familiar has become unfamiliar. This is an unavoidable stop along the road of transition—welcome to the abyss.

Stage Three—The Abyss

I remember this pit stop vividly as the Lord was healing me and removing bondages. It was a peculiar I-don't-know-who-I-am-anymore place where everything I knew was no longer. *I* was no longer. The abyss is that place when you are no longer your old self, but not yet your new self either. It is an almost indefinable place—a no man's land. How do you feel? *Blah.* You have come through feeling grief, and now you just feel kind of . . . nothing. It is like a dark, empty, weird state of nothingness—*blah.*

An abyss, by definition, is a bottomless gulf, a deep pit or great space. That sounds about right, huh? When you hit it, you will know what I am talking about. I felt lost, like a shell of a person with no insides. I started wondering how long I would be in this blah state and if the Lord was going to leave me like this forever. I started to feel nervous that I had lost my old self, and even though I did not want to stay my old self, the old self was better than this place of "no self."

When I asked friends at church about this, no one had answers for me. Maybe those I talked to had not gone into this realm of surrender with the Lord. All I know is that every single person I have worked with, counseled and stood by through their healing process has encountered this stage. When it comes to deep healing, the abyss is an inevitable stage, and there is no way around it. The only way *to* is *through.*

In the abyss, you need reassurance that you are heading in the right direction, and affirmation that you are on the brink of change. This is where pressure kicks in. You may have an overwhelming drive to grab onto something, anything that gives you a sense of self. There will be great temptation to go back to the familiar but it is imperative that you ride it out, take your hands off the controls and stay the course! Train yourself to stay where it is uncomfortable. This is where the warfare begins.

Stage Four—Warfare

In the book of Exodus, God made a promise to deliver the Israelites from slavery and bring them into the Promised Land that was flowing with all sorts of good things. They could not wait to get there. They began their journey full of hope, but it wasn't long before it started getting hard, they started getting tired and the Promised Land seemed more like a faint idea than a reality. The Bible calls this the wilderness. The wilderness is a lot like the abyss. It is in the middle of nowhere, dry and dead. It is where the Israelites lost their excitement, and their desire for the Promised Land began to wane. The reality of freedom felt far off, and the memory of slavery began to get distorted. They thought: *I'm not sure about freedom; all I know is I'm out here in the middle of nowhere. Am I really going to make it? I'm not even sure what the Promised Land holds or how long it will take for me to get there, but I do know that if I turn back now, at least I'll have food to eat and a bed to sleep in. Slavery wasn't really that bad. Look at me now, trusting God for what? For this? For nothing?*

This is warfare. When we are in our abyss, our wilderness, these are the same kinds of thoughts we have. These thoughts are warfare against us moving forward and having all God says we can have. We are tempted to go back to what is familiar. The Israelites had to go through a season of having nothing before they came into everything, and so do we. Some of our most uncomfortable times occur right before change. That is when we must make the decision to stay where it is uncomfortable and not turn back. It is not easy. Transition times can be difficult and uncomfortable. There will come a time when it becomes so difficult that you regret letting go. You wonder if you did the right thing. This will *always* happen so expect it! Do not be surprised. See it for what it is: a form of warfare from the enemy. He will make you question your decision and tempt you to take matters into your own hands. You will want to go back to what is familiar instead of waiting on the Lord to come through.

You might have heard the expression, "The Lord is never early, but He is always on time." Our God likes to come through in the final hour. Why does He do that? Is the Lord holding out on us? No, there is a reason for the wilderness season. It builds our faith. It is where we learn what it really means to trust in the Lord, and how to wait on Him. Waiting produces dependence on Him like nothing else can.

While in transition, it is common to think negative thoughts: *It's so hard. It's too much work. My life was so much better before.* First of all, yes, it is hard, but do not make it harder. It does take some effort to go through this process, but anything worth having takes dedication. It will be hard, but staying in bondage is harder. It will hurt, but living enslaved hurts more. And truthfully, thoughts such as "my life was so much better before God" or "my life was so much better before I sacrificed and was left here to die in the wilderness" are big enemy lies with a capital *L*—Lies! Thoughts like those are an enemy tactic to convince us that we were so much better off before, that our struggles were not really that severe. We may question ourselves. *Maybe I exaggerated how much that person I let go of mistreated me. Was the drinking and partying really that bad?* We are lured into believing that our binging and purging was not that big of a deal. It was not truly slavery, was it? After all, we tell ourselves, "It is not like I did it every day."

Do not be fooled! If things were so much better before, you would not be desperately searching for freedom. Things were *not* better before, but they *will* get better if you hold fast and keep moving forward. Are you willing to stay the course and be uncomfortable? The road to freedom has some bumps and the wilderness will hurt, but the season is temporary—slavery is permanent.

Stage Five—The Promise

If you do not turn back, but stay with it, in due time and season, your old ways, old thoughts and old life will pass away. You will be amazed at your transformation. God is faithful, and when we stay tethered to Him, He will bring us into our personal Promised Land that flows with milk and honey. We will get a taste of real life and what it means to be free.

If the Son makes you free, you shall be free indeed.

John 8:36

15

Fruits

Problems are not stop signs, they are guidelines.

Robert H. Schuller

The Bible teaches us that one way we identify someone or something is by the fruit, meaning a result, product or consequence. In the natural realm, we recognize an orange tree because it produces oranges. Likewise, in regard to spiritual things, we are able to discern what is godly and what is ungodly by the fruit it produces. Take our thoughts for example. When we ruminate on the negative circumstances of our life, we produce the fruits of hopelessness and anxiety. When we keep our mind fixed on the Lord, we reap the fruit of peace. Or, in regard to our actions, when we sin we reap the fruit of death, because the wages of sin is death (see Romans 6:23). Counterfeit comforts are fruits also—they are the products of unhealthy roots that develop into addictions and compulsive behaviors. The way they manifest is different for each of us, but regardless of the vice in which they surface, all counterfeit comforts are fruits of roots—roots of wounds, hurts and unresolved issues.

One of the damaging behaviors I dealt with was bulimia. Bulimia, the act of binging and purging, appears to stem from a desire to be thin, but the roots go much deeper than that and can have less to do with food than we might believe. Bulimia is often a destructive avenue for dealing with feelings. Anyone who has binged knows that no matter what you eat or how much you eat, you cannot get satisfied. Nothing hits the spot. Even as your stomach is beginning to get full, you still crave. Regardless of how much you eat, the desperation for more food intensifies, but the food does not fill the void inside of you. You can be so full that you are sick to your stomach, but you still feel empty. That is because the hole that is crying out to be filled is not the stomach. The purging of the food deals with another aspect of the cycle. One might not consciously realize the connection between purging food and purging emotions, but when the food is purged, it brings with it a release. It is as if all the pent up hurt, anger and frustration that has been stuffed down comes up and out. Purging is a symbolic and literal lifting of burden and pressure, a lightening of the load—until the cycle begins again.

Another example, something that I have not personally dealt with but has become prevalent, especially with the younger generation, is a form of self-mutilation called cutting. Knives or razor blades are used to cut into various parts of the body, such as arms, legs and stomach. Cutting has actually been around since biblical days. The gospel of Mark gives an example of a tormented man who cut himself:

> And always, night and day, he was in the mountains and in the tombs, crying out and cutting himself with stones.
>
> Mark 5:5

Cutting can bring an emotional release just like vomiting. It is as though you are able to get rid of something and alleviate built-up pressure. With the release of pressure comes a sense of rest and well-being. For those who have shut down emotionally as a survival mechanism to deal with trauma, the pain brought on by cutting can actually be a relief. It grants the person a sense of peace and normalcy that they are able to feel at all. Being able to feel anything, even pain, is comforting to those who are so numb and disconnected that they go through life feeling absolutely nothing.

Another destructive behavior we are hearing more about is hoarding. Hoarding is the term given to those who store such massive amounts of items in their home that there is no room left for living. They surround themselves with clothes and other various items from floor to ceiling until there is little space left to walk, sit or sleep. Another version of hoarding is using animals to replace possessions. People can have literally hundreds of animals with them in their home, living in the midst of chaos and excrement. Hoarding has nothing to do with the desire to shop, accumulate possessions or greed for more things. Nor does it have to do with a love for animals. Behind hoarding is always an emotional issue like losing a loved one or a traumatic event of some kind. Hoarding meets an emotional need and offers a sense of control, comfort and security.

I recently heard a story about an emerging trend among those who had undergone gastric bypass surgery. Doctors reported that many of their patients, now unable to consume very much food, were drinking large quantities of alcohol, some as many as ten martinis a day! What a clear example of a counterfeit comfort! Overeating was not the crux of the problem for these people. It appeared so by looking at their bodies, but the weight was merely the fruit of a deeper issue.

Remove the food without addressing the root, and comfort is sought through an alternative vice.

I saw the same dynamic in my own life regarding my relationship with food. My obsessive dieting was not helping me for any length of time, because food was not the problem. It was merely a fruit in my life that reflected an unhealthy root. So there I was, a tree with a withered branch, spending all my time focusing on my branch and my fruit . . . maybe if I exercised more, cut out certain food groups or tried the latest Hollywood diet. . . . I would think about my branch constantly. *What should I eat? How much should I eat? What time should I eat?* Then I would pray about my branch. "Lord, help me to not overeat. Please give me self-control." But nothing was healing my branch! I realized that my branch was dying because of a root in me that was not healthy. In order to heal my branch, I had to go to the source of the problem—the root. Healthy roots produce healthy branches and good fruit. That is how it works in nature, and that is how it works with us. That is why the Spirit of the Lord instructed me not to dwell on the food, but to deal with the root, and in doing so, my food problem would take care of itself.

It is such a relief to no longer be bound by "good" food or "bad" food. Do not get me wrong. If we live on nothing but mashed potatoes and ice cream we probably will not feel or look as good as we could, but those foods are not bad, and they are not the reason for our struggle. To be clear, if we choose to exclude certain foods from our diet because we do not like or enjoy them, or because our body does not respond favorably to them, that is one thing. Of course we are free to do that. What I am talking about here is avoiding foods out of fear—God is not in that.

We cannot find freedom by trying to change from the outside in! When we do not understand that the root is the problem, and we endeavor to change our fruit by the strength of our will, we will always fall short. Then we get caught in a trap of frustration and condemnation. Why can't I stop this? Why can't I change? Paul had the same struggles:

> For what I am doing, I do not understand. For what I will to do, that I do not practice; but what I hate, that I do. If, then, I do what I will not to do, I agree with the law that it is good. But now, it is no longer I who do it, but sin that dwells in me. For I know that in me (that is, in my flesh) nothing good dwells; for to will is present with me, but how to perform what is good I do not find. For the good that I will to do, I do not do; but the evil I will not to do, that I practice.
>
> Romans 7:15–19

Yes, there are times when we have to take a stand and say no to the flesh, but the problem is that sometimes our problem is more than just a decision of the will. It is deeper than that. There are areas in us that run so deep, that as hard as we try, we just cannot change our fruit or ourselves. That is why we must begin at the root.

The Lord is not as concerned with your fruits as you might think. That might sound shocking and anti-scriptural, but let me say it like this: The Lord is actually more interested in our roots. He is not judging our behavior as much as we might think. He knows that at times our behavior does not line up with who we truly are, not because we are disobedient sinners, but because of our wounds.

Sometimes our fruit does not reflect our heart but is a product of our hurt.

The truth is that for many of us our actions do not always line up with our morals and our beliefs. This is not because we are being willfully disobedient, but because our need for love and comfort can override our values and trump our beliefs.

We are not purposefully rebelling against God. We are a hurting people doing the best we can. Those around us might be judging, but God is not judging us as much as we might think He is, or at least, not in the way we think He is. God looks at our motives. Our Lord sees through our behavior and into our hearts. That is why He can love someone like David from the Bible so dearly even though David made huge mistakes. David had a man killed and the Father still called him "a man after His own heart" (1 Samuel 13:14). That should give you some peace regarding where you have fallen short. Do not get me wrong, I am not saying that our actions do not matter or have consequences. Paul expresses this clearly when he states that grace does not give us a license to sin:

> What shall we say then? Shall we continue in sin that grace may abound? Certainly not! How shall we who died to sin live any longer in it?
>
> Romans 6:1–2

What I am talking about here is that God looks at our hearts, and He has a lot of grace for us as we are growing. If you are reading this book, then you are a seeker. You are someone who has a heart for God and a desire to live in His will and in His ways. What is wonderful about God is that we do not have to be perfect before coming to Him. He will take us just the way we are. He is not disappointed in us. He is focused on loving us back to health and healing our deep wounds. He knows once our roots are tended to, our fruits will reflect that. To receive healing, we need to go beyond the surface symptoms and deal with the roots.

16

Roots

If the root is holy, so are the branches.

Romans 11:16

Uncovering the Roots

God works with us from the inside out. If what is going on deep within us is sound, then our outer life reflects that. Sickly roots—wounds and unresolved hurts—produce unhealthy branches that bear the fruit of counterfeit comforts in our life. As we delve below the surface and uncover the roots behind our destructive patterns of behavior, healing begins. Let's explore some of the more common and universal roots beneath counterfeit comforts.

The Root of Rejection and Abandonment

Relationships are extremely effective in exposing roots. Any-time we have a strong emotional reaction it is a signal that there is an area in us being triggered, and there is nothing like other people to elicit a strong emotional reaction! Our most intimate relationships, like marriage, are God ordained to do just that. But even a more casual encounter, like a first date, can provoke reactions in us that we might not expect. Although the following illustration is hypothetical, truth be told, I have lived this scenario in various forms myself. If you have spent much time as a single adult in the dating world, you might relate as well.

You are asked out on a date, and you decide to go. About fifteen minutes into the date, you realize that you are not into it, but the night is young so you decide to make the most of it. You embark on the usual getting to know you chitchat: where you grew up, what you do for a living, if you like sushi . . . yada, yada. You are biding time until the date is over and you can go home, jump into your PJs and watch some TV. As the evening is nearing its end, you begin thinking, *What if this guy tries to kiss me? He's nice and everything, but I really hope he doesn't try to kiss me.*

Finally, you make it to your door, say thanks for the night and are able to avoid the kiss. As you are getting ready for bed you decide that when he calls, you are definitely not going to go out with him again. You start running the conversation over in your mind about what you will say when he calls; how to be nice about it, and in the most gentle of ways let him know that you just don't think the two of you are heading in the romantic direction.

The next day comes and goes—no phone call. You are kind of relieved. Then another day passes. You start to think, *Hmm, I'm surprised he hasn't called yet.* You check your phone to see if it is working. Then another day comes and goes and you wonder, *Why isn't he calling me? I know I wasn't interested in him, but I wanted to be the one to say I wasn't interested.* A full week passes, and you are now officially obsessed and checking your phone every three minutes for a missed call or text. You have run through the date in your mind a hundred times, questioning what you said, what you did, what you ate, how you ate. You are turning every possible scenario over and over in your mind: *What did I do wrong? Am I not pretty enough? Did I say something stupid? Why didn't he like me? What's wrong with me?*

The initial, slight tinge of sadness at the beginning of the week has now escalated into full-blown depression. Obviously, something deeper is going on here to be this wrought-up over a guy you did not even connect with. When the reaction is far greater than what actually happened, it is what I call a "punishment doesn't fit the crime" response; the feelings are far more extreme than the event warranted. In this case, the situation had little to do with the guy. He merely triggered a familiar place of feeling unloved, unwanted and cast aside. This event poked a long-standing wound that runs deep: a root of rejection.

How does the root of rejection become established? There are myriad ways, divorce in your family being one of them. Many of us nowadays come from broken homes where parents separated or one parent abandoned the family. When a parent leaves, we as children question ourselves, not consciously, but subconsciously: *Why would they do that if I was lovable? What did I do to make this happen? What is wrong with me?* Rejection can even be rooted when two parents stay together, but are not necessarily present in heart and spirit in the family. They may be present in the physical, but not available emotionally, so on some level there is a feeling of aloneness and abandonment. When the primary people who are supposed to support us both physically and emotionally do not provide that security, it leaves a lasting mark.

A root of rejection can form in several other ways. Perhaps it was made clear to you that you were a financial burden, an accidental birth or not the sex that your parents desired. Hearing or even sensing a parent's disappointment can instill a deep root of rejection, leaving you feeling unwanted and burdensome. Rejection can even germinate while a child is in the womb. There might have been talk about aborting you, or you were born and then given up for adoption. In the case of adoption, regardless of the reasoning of the parent, and no matter how justified those reasons might be, the root of rejection can run deep in the child who was given up. Core beliefs may be formed, such as *I must be unlovable if I was given away. There has to be something intrinsically wrong with me for my own parents not to want me.* This is not to place blame or guilt on parents that gave up children for adoption, but merely to understand that deep-seated, core beliefs can be produced from those situations. The Lord can heal all sides of this: the guilt and sorrow of the parent and the wounds of abandonment for the child.

The Root of Grief and Despair from Loss

I was moved by the story of a beautiful English woman I met who was in her fifties. Her father passed away when she was ten years old. She came home from school, and was told that her father had died that day. She attended his funeral a few days later. After the service, her dad was never mentioned in her home again. She was not asked how she felt. There were no memories of him shared. It was as if her father had never existed. It is no surprise that at thirteen she started drinking beer and smoking cigarettes. As her story evolved, so did the level of her alcohol and drug use. She quickly progressed from beer to hard alcohol and from cigarettes to cocaine. It was not until decades later when she hit bottom and got sober that she began to connect her drinking and drug use to her repressed grief of losing her father.

Millions of people share a story like hers. Listening to her reminded me of the films *Walk the Line*, the story of Johnny Cash, and *Ray*, about the life of Ray Charles. Both incredibly gifted musicians were devastated by the loss of a brother at a young age. Throughout the movies, despair, drugs and alcohol enslaved both Johnny Cash and Ray Charles. The films unfolded with scene after scene of them drinking and drugging, interspersed with flashbacks of them reliving the moment when they lost their brothers. Here were two men whose lives were shattered because of overwhelming feelings they did not know what to do with. They could not process what had happened to them, so they spent their lives trying to escape the tormenting memories of loss.

Why do people we love die? I do not know all the answers, but I do know that it is a crafty move by the enemy to coerce us into turning against God and distancing ourselves emotionally from the Lord when we need Him most. God is not to blame. We need to put blame where blame is due, and direct our animosity toward the true culprit: the adversary. God does not cause these situations; these devastating losses are not from Him to teach us a lesson. Yes, we can be strengthened through trials, but God does not put us in heart-wrenching situations for us to learn a lesson or for us to grow. Nevertheless, He can and will use everything we go through if we put our trust in Him.

And we know that all things work together for good to those who love God, to those who are the called according to His purpose.

Romans 8:28

The Root of Shame

Much of the tribulation we endure, including all forms of abuse—physical, emotional, mental or sexual—leaves us with a gnawing sense that something is inherently wrong with us.

That is shame. For some, the shame is all-encompassing: shame to breathe, shame to take up space, shame to simply *be*. This is especially prevalent if the abuse was suffered when you were a child. Children often do not have the maturity or understanding to process the severity of what is happening to them, so they sometimes turn the blame inward, believing they are wrong or bad. Countless studies show that, in their minds, children themselves believe they are the reason for the abuse.

Abuse in every form is devastating, but sexual abuse is especially confusing. While physical and emotional abuse, such as hitting, threatening or berating never feel good, we are created by God to experience sexual interaction as something that does feel good. When there is sexual abuse, the heart and mind know something is wrong, that there is a violation happening; but simultaneously, the body might still react favorably. This does not make sense for anyone, especially for a young mind. Feelings of pleasure mixed with guilt, shame and anger cause confusion in the child. When sexuality is misused and imposed, the result is often self-hatred and shame.

Getting to the root of shame by purposefully searching out the source of those feelings in an on-the-floor-type scenario is difficult and seems counterintuitive. Doing so will not come naturally or easily; it might be one of the hardest things you ever have to do. When you have spent your whole life trying to distance yourself from the shame, the last thing you want to do is deliberately go right back into the middle of it. Shame runs deep and is so painful to experience because it goes to the core of who you think you are. Intertwined within you may be feelings of humiliation and embarrassment, and a sense of being dirty. When you have felt that way your entire life, and have done everything you could *not* to feel that way, jumping head first into such negative territory feels both foreign and absolutely unnatural.

The first step is to be willing. The second is to be brave and courageous, and know that the Lord is with you. The third is to recognize that your healing lies in facing what you have not wanted ever to face again by feeling what you have not wanted to feel. It might help you to know that those feelings *are not you*. Feeling dirty is not the truth about who you are, but it is blocking you from experiencing all of who you are. Remember, you are dealing with what is controlling you—not with what is inherently you—and it is time for you to get your life back.

To receive healing, you must uncover the lies that have been built up in your mind. You will find wrong beliefs at the root. Thoughts, such as:

No one loves me.

I am alone.

No one will ever take care of me.

I am worthless.

I am dumb.

I am unlovable.

Something is wrong with me.

I am not okay.

All roots have these kinds of lies associated with them, and when our experience lines up with the lies, we believe them. The untruths are so familiar, and they are all we have ever known. It is as though our wiring is off, and we operate based on what we have experienced—on *our* truth as opposed to *the* truth. These lies produce the fruit of shame and feeling horribly about ourselves. They drive us to overeat, turn to alcohol, or excessively shop so that we do not have to feel our own hatred of ourselves. But the truth is, we are running from the lies. The lies feel real, and though circumstances may seem to confirm that they are real, they are not true.

The only thing that is true is what God says about me.

Much healing comes when we identify and expose the falsehoods that tell us we are to blame, we are faulty and we are shameful. When the Lord comes in to uncover deeply held wrong beliefs, and we learn how to renew our minds in an area of wounding, we begin to see transformation.

When we learn the truth we can say with confidence, "I am not what has happened to me. I am not what others have done to me or said to me, and I am not what I have thought about myself. I am only who God says that I am: I am fearfully and wonderfully made (see Psalm 139:14). He chose me before the foundation of the world; I am His adopted child who is holy and blameless in His sight" (see Ephesians 1:4).

It is through uncovering the lies and replacing them with truth that we begin to live within the place where we know the truth and the truth makes us free (see John 8:32). The truth alone does not make us free. It is the truth we *know* that makes us free. It takes time, a lot of truth and a lot of God's love to uproot what has been planted. Only He can change us, and when we are willing to submit our lives to Him, He truly can be our Healer.

Some extremely sensitive issues have been touched upon within the last two chapters as we have explored fruits and roots. These topics are not to be taken lightly and cannot be thoroughly fleshed out in a paragraph or two. There is a lot to know about these various actions and addictions, and each individual has their own set of complex circumstances that could drive them into these various behaviors. I am not intending to simplify the issue by saying that repressed feelings are the only culprit or that you should just feel your feelings and all will be fine. There are many components in play, but *one* of them *is* repressed emotions and a response to trauma that has not been processed in a healthy way. This may not be the whole answer, but it is a place to start, and a piece of the puzzle toward wholeness.

After years of experience in ministering to people, working through my own deep emotional wounds and witnessing God's healing power in my life and the lives of others, I know that healing and freedom are possible. And I know they are possible for you! The examples stated here have been with the intention of helping you clarify what some of your roots might be, and what could be behind some of the behaviors that you cannot seem to control. Not being a professional clinician, I am offering you biblical solutions, and what the Lord has taught me. My prayer for you is that these writings, along with the Holy Spirit, will spark something in you and awaken your understanding, so that you might be able to connect some dots as to who you are, and why you do what you do. I do not have all of your answers. It is up to the Holy Spirit to reveal to you personally all the intricacies of your individual experience and life. One thing I do know for sure is regardless of what you have gone through, as you allow the Lord into those deep places, healing can be found. You have to be willing to get in there with God, get into His presence, get on-the-floor and seek connection with yourself and with Him. Time does not heal all wounds, but God *does* heal all wounds. He can, and He will.

"I have heard your prayer, I have seen your tears; surely I will heal you."

2 Kings 20:5

17

Rewired

There are far, far better things ahead
than any we leave behind.

C. S. Lewis

*A*s I continued spending time on-the-floor practicing God's presence, the Holy Spirit began exposing my own roots to me. He revealed why I ran to food as my counterfeit comfort and what was going on with me beneath the surface. In addition to my tumultuous relationship with food and my body, another area I struggled in was romantic relationships. I always seemed to pick the wrong guy and had a pattern of bad relationships that were emotionally devastating. I often found myself with a man who said he loved me, and I knew he did genuinely care about me, but his behavior would contradict his words. He would profess love, but down the road I would find out he had lied, cheated or betrayed my trust in some way. No matter how the relationship started, regardless of what man I chose, the relationship unfolded the same way, time and time again. I took this before the Lord and asked, "What is up with this? Show me what is going on here."

I had adhered to a common, worldly perspective that the issue was with the men I was choosing, and if only I could find the "right" man then everything would be different. In prayer, the Lord showed me something different entirely. He made it clear that this pattern had nothing to do with choosing the right man; it had to do with a root inside of me that needed healing. He told me, *The way you have love wired is off.* I pondered that, and as I continued to seek Him for deeper understanding, He began to remind me of my upbringing. My parents got divorced when I was two years old. I lived with my mother and saw my father only a handful of times throughout the year. As a little girl, I would get so excited and worked up prior to my dad's visits. Before he arrived, I would plant myself near the front door and ask incessantly, "Where is Daddy? Is he here yet? Is he here yet?" I was too young to remember, but was told later that my dad would often be so late in getting me that my excitement would morph into anger, frustration and, eventually, tears. After frantically running around the house looking for him for hours, I would finally wear myself out and fall asleep. I was too young to consciously remember this, but regardless, it had a lasting impact on me.

The dynamic with my mother was different. Unlike my father, she was always there physically to care for my needs. She was also consistent verbally in her love for me, always telling me that she adored me and that I was smart, beautiful and special. But when I was eleven years old, out of nowhere, I was told that I was going to go live with my dad. It was abrupt and shocking. I did not even really know my dad. My mom had reasons behind this choice, but as a child, I was not able to process those reasons and make sense of them. I felt like I was being given away.

As the Lord brought these scenarios with my parents back to the forefront of my mind, I saw a pattern that had been established from childhood. I had an *aha* moment. My dad *said* he loved me, but he didn't show up for me in the way I needed. My mom *said* she loved me, but from my perspective her actions did not back up her words. Both of these experiences, among others, formed what I believed love to be: saying one thing and doing another. That became my "love story" that played out over and over. As a young adult, interestingly enough, every relationship I had with a man that felt like love was interwoven with this same dynamic. There would be plenty of verbal affirmation, but little follow-through in action. It didn't matter if the guy was an athlete or an actor, rich or poor, conservative or eclectic. Beyond who they were or what they did, I was somehow always drawn to the guy who said one thing and did another. I was wired to believe that that was love, so when I encountered that kind of treatment, it felt like love to me. It was familiar.

The Lord spoke to my spirit that it was this specific wiring that blocked me from having the kind of real love I was longing for. I would never find the "right" man because what felt right to me was not right, and what felt true to me, was not true. The Lord said, *Spend time with Me. I am Love, and I will show you what real love is, what it feels like and what it does. I will be faithful to you. I am not a man that I should lie* (see Numbers 23:19). *I do what I say and say what I do. As you spend time with Me, I will rewire what you believe love to be, so as you encounter love that says one thing and does another, it will no longer ring true as love to you. I will rewire you, so that what has been familiar to you will become unfamiliar, and what has been unfamiliar will become familiar. Then, when you have a proper understanding of what real love is, who you are drawn to, and who is drawn to you, will change.*

He showed me that I could have a relationship that reflected real love only after He taught me what real love looked like, felt like and acted like, and that love is more than just intense feelings. Real love, agape love, the God-kind of love includes commitment, loyalty and steadfastness. It is sacrificial, esteems others over itself, and is long-suffering, gentle, kind and honest. What the Word and the Spirit of the Lord were teaching me about love was very different from what I had grown up with and what I had seen in the movies. I thought love was all about intensity and passion. Do not get me wrong; there is nothing wrong with passion. Passion is a good thing, but there are a lot more ingredients and qualities that go into making a solid relationship than passionate feelings alone.

In time, when the Lord had rewired me and that false association was broken in me, I attracted a different kind of man. When I first met him there was a connection, but it felt a little different. He was outside my usual modus operandi. He was solid and steadfast in a way I had never experienced. Even when I got upset or was harsh toward him, he didn't go anywhere. He loved me even when I was not that lovely or loveable. Prior to him, men would say they loved me, but at the first sign of conflict they would be out the door. When conflict arose with this man, he stood strong. The pivotal moment in our relationship came during a fight between us. I was really upset and a lot of junk was spewing out of my mouth. It was directed at him and not very nice. He responded with, "I love you, and I am not going anywhere. You can try to push me away, but it won't work. I know when you get angry and upset that *that* is not who you really are." I am not sure if he realized just how Christ-like he was acting toward me, but he was the living version of Proverbs 15:1 which says, "A soft answer turns away wrath." He was so gentle and loving in response to my anger that it melted me. I had never felt so loved. Two years later, he became my husband. One of the things he spoke to me on our wedding day during his vows was, "I was made to love you." And he was, but the Lord had to do an internal work in me first to prepare me to be able to receive that love. I am so glad He did.

These series of experiences I had with the Lord were monumental and life changing. He continued to speak to me and meet me on-the-floor. There were times when I got up off the floor and felt as if a little hole in my heart and soul was mended. I was not completely healed, but a piece of me that was missing had been filled in, and a part of me that was wounded had received His soothing balm. Over time, as if I were Humpty Dumpty, He started putting me back together again. It was the time I spent in His presence that made all the difference.

God heals and changes us in a way that is very real, but somewhat intangible. How it comes to pass can be difficult to understand, yet Scripture tells us that we are not to try to figure things out through reasoning, because the carnal mind is the enemy to the ways of God.

The carnal mind is enmity against God.

Romans 8:7

Often God's ways cannot be seen with the naked eye. We do not see the wind, but we see the effects after a strong wind has passed through. Likewise, we cannot always see the power of the Lord, but we can see the effects after He has touched our lives. God knows what He is doing. We do not need to understand every aspect because that is not our job. He is the Potter, and we are the clay, and the clay does not tell the Potter what to make and how to make it. Spiritual things cannot be discerned through our limited understanding. His ways are higher and cannot be fully explained.

"For My thoughts are not your thoughts, nor are your ways My ways," says the LORD. "For as the heavens are higher than the earth, so are My ways higher than your ways, and My thoughts than your thoughts."

Isaiah 55:8–9

Often we find ourselves striving to understand everything when what we really need to do is trust. Sometimes it is best to release control and let go of needing to know every facet of what God is doing. Our God is a loving God. His ways work, and we can trust Him.

Trust in the LORD with all your heart, and lean not on your own understanding; in all your ways acknowledge Him, and He shall direct your paths.

Proverbs 3:5–6

We cannot figure out how God does everything; His ways are too vast for us. With God, our understanding is often on a need-to-know basis, and there is a lot less that we need to know than we think! All we need to know is the One who knows everything, and trust in Him to get us where we need to go. Step out in faith, and trust the One who knows. When the Lord is involved, the result will be better than you think—far greater than what you could even imagine.

Never be afraid to trust an unknown future to a known God.

Corrie ten Boom

18

Tools for Transformation

The Bible was not given for our information
but for our transformation.

D. L. Moody

*I*ntimacy with the Lord is what produces lasting change. Time in His presence, along with a clear understanding of how He has equipped us to be free and victorious, makes all the difference. The answers we seek are found in the Bible. The Word of God is a practical manual full of wisdom and instruction.

B.I.B.L.E—Basic Instructions Before Leaving Earth

God is all about providing us with tools to fight the battle and win. One of the tools He has given us is "the sword of the Spirit, which is the word of God" (Ephesians 6:17). When we become Christians, we are all given the same sword, but mastery of the sword is up to us. Lack of mastery is not usually from lack of desire but due to a lack of knowledge and understanding.

> My people are destroyed for lack of knowledge.
>
> Hosea 4:6

> Get wisdom! Get understanding! Do not forget, nor turn away from the words of my mouth. Do not forsake her, and she will preserve you; love her, and she will keep you. Wisdom is the principal thing; therefore get wisdom. And in all your getting, get understanding.
>
> Proverbs 4:5–7

It always comes down to wisdom, knowledge and understanding. The Lord does not hold us accountable for what we do not know, but what we do not know *can* hurt us. You will be surprised at the success you achieve when you know the tools you have been given and you become proficient in using them. Amazing changes in your life will result. God is so good that we do not have to look far for the tools we need. They are at our disposal, ready for use and with us wherever we go. He made them a part of us so we literally cannot leave home without them. The first tool I am talking about starts at the top and is built right into our heads: our mind.

> Do not be conformed to this world, but be transformed by the renewing of your mind.
>
> Romans 12:2

Many of us are familiar with this Scripture, but how do we implement it? What does renewing our mind look like in everyday life? Do I renew my mind by reading the Word and going to church? Well, yes and no. You can go to church every day and not have a renewed mind. Just hearing a sermon or attending a Bible study does not necessarily equate to a renewed mind. There is more to it than that.

To be "conformed to this world" is to think the thoughts the ruler of this world gives us. In order to have the mind of Christ (see 1 Corinthians 2:16) and be renewed in the spirit of our mind (see Ephesians 4:23), we must align our thoughts with God's thoughts. We do that by identifying a wrong thought, which is a lie or an enemy thought, and replacing that lie with the truth. If you study Romans 12:2 in the original Greek, one of the translations for renew is replace; therefore, one way we renew our mind is by replacing our thoughts. We renew our mind by replacing worldly thoughts with godly thoughts, replacing lies with thoughts that align with the nature and Spirit of God and His Word.

Think Effectively

In the chapter titled "Do Not Believe Everything You Think," we covered how the battle is in the mind and how to take thoughts captive. That is spiritual warfare. But there is a time when we are not in warfare that we can train our mind to think effectively. We do this by practicing purposeful thinking.

Purposeful Thinking

The average person thinks whatever breezes into his or her mind. They think according to how they feel and according to their circumstances. A spiritual person thinks differently. We who are spiritual practice purposeful thinking and intentionally *choose* to put our mind on the truth of the Word of God, regardless of how we feel and what is going on around us. We choose to think about what is true over what is fact, and the good news is, we can choose to do this at any time throughout the day.

For example, the fact might be that finances are tight. It is easy to focus on that but if you do, before you know it, you are consumed with fear and anxiety. The dollar amount in your bank account is surely a fact, but the truth is that the Lord will supply all your need according to His riches and glory by Christ Jesus (see Philippians 4:19). The more we focus on the circumstances and the facts, the more we root them as truths into our mind and heart. The more we think on truths from the Word, the more those truths become rooted into our mind and heart. The more we focus on the truth of the Word, the more peace we have. Peace does not have to be a random occurrence or dictated by our circumstances—peace and joy when things are good, torment and unrest when things are bad. In God, we can have peace regardless of what is going on in our lives because our peace does not come from what is happening externally.

> Peace is not a direct result of our circumstances, but how we choose to think on our circumstances.

Peace is one of the fruits of the Spirit: "But the fruit of the Spirit is love, joy, **peace,** longsuffering, kindness, goodness, faithfulness, gentleness, self-control" (Galatians 5:22–23).

Jesus Himself is called the Prince of Peace. Peace is available to all believers and a promise from the Lord for all Christians, but it is not just handed to us when we believe in Him and are saved. If it were, we would all be at peace all the time. Like all of God's promises, we do not automatically receive them upon salvation. They are available to us, but we must learn how to appropriate them.

We are often under the assumption that if God wanted us to have certain things, we would just have them. Nothing in the Kingdom works that way. It is like saying, "If God wanted me to have a good marriage, I would." We are all aware of how important the covenant of marriage is to the Lord. It is a given that He wants us to have good marriages, but the quality of our marriage comes down to knowing and applying certain skills and tools. The degree in which we are willing to go to be intimate, deal with conflict, communicate and esteem our spouse above ourselves, determines the kind of marriage we will have. Just being a Christian does not automatically guarantee us a good marriage, and just being a Christian does not automatically guarantee that we will walk in all the blessings available to us. God desires for us to have many things, but as believers, it is our responsibility to learn how to use the tools He has given us to obtain all He has for us. The Bible teaches us that peace is a fruit of the Spirit granted to us by using the tool of our mind. Our level of peace is determined by *how* we think and what we *choose* to think.

> You will keep him in perfect peace, whose mind is stayed on You.
>
> Isaiah 26:3

Meditate on These Things

Finally, brethren, whatever things are true, whatever things are noble, whatever things are just, whatever things are pure, whatever things are lovely, whatever things are of good report, if there is any virtue and if there is anything praiseworthy— meditate on these things. The things which you learned and received and heard and saw in me, these do, and the God of peace will be with you.

> Philippians 4:8–9

Peace comes when we think on things that are good, pure and praiseworthy. Regardless of what we are going through there is *always* at least one thing in our lives that is praiseworthy. Always! In Philippians chapter four, Paul instructs us to meditate on these things. So, what does it mean to meditate? How do we do it?

When we hear the word meditate nowadays, we often think of Eastern religions where you sit cross-legged, and try to empty your mind while chanting a mantra. Transcendental Meditation, as it is called, is very different from how the Bible instructs Christians to meditate. The Word is full of Scriptures commanding us to meditate on God's ways and His works within our own hearts.

> This Book of the Law shall not depart from your mouth, but you shall **meditate** in it day and night, that you may observe to do according to all that is written in it. For then you will make your way prosperous, and then you will have good success.
>
> Joshua 1:8

> I will also **meditate** on all Your work, and talk of Your deeds.
>
> Psalm 77:12

> I will **meditate** on Your precepts, and contemplate Your ways.
>
> Psalm 119:15

When we meditate as Christians, we do not attempt to empty our minds but just the opposite: We focus our minds on the Word of God. To *meditate* means to "ruminate" or "to mull over." The Hebrew word translated into English as *meditate* literally means "chew the cud." Chewing the cud is something that a cow does. A cow has four stomachs. When a cow eats grass and swallows it, the grass goes into the first stomach. The cow then regurgitates the grass into its mouth to chew it some more. The regurgitation is called the cud. The cow continues chewing the cud, swallowing, regurgitating and chewing some more until the food makes it into the fourth stomach. Not to be graphic, but that is a good example of how to meditate as

Christians according to Scripture. We take a verse and mull it over. We chew on it, swallow it, then bring it up again, and roll it over in our mind and heart some more. A cow chews its cud so that every possible nutrient can be broken down into digestible components for it to use to continue to live and to stay healthy. We chew and meditate on God's Word for the same reasons: spiritual life and health.

Meditating is not a difficult skill to learn. Little do we realize we are actually meditating all the time. We are experts at turning things over and over in our minds, always ruminating on something, right? Sounds a lot like worrying. If you know how to worry, you know how to meditate. The question then becomes not *if* we are meditating, but *what* we are meditating on. If you find yourself feeling depressed, anxious or worried, consider what you are thinking about.

Think About What You Are Thinking About

Feelings follow thoughts.

Negative feelings are often the fruit of an abundance of negative thinking. Meditating on the cares of the world and negative circumstances reaps the fruit of anxiety, stress and hopelessness. Meditating on what is praiseworthy reaps the fruit of joy and peace. Here is a simple, practical example: Right now, I can stop what I am doing and spend five minutes focusing on what I consider to be my husband's not-so-favorable qualities. After five minutes, I would most likely find myself feeling extremely negative and resentful toward him. I might even begin to question my marriage and wonder why I married this guy in the first place! Or I can do the opposite and spend five minutes thinking about certain aspects of my husband that I absolutely adore and special times we have spent together. I can reminisce over our wedding day, how beautiful it is to watch him playing with our daughter or simply how cute his hair looks in the morning. After a few minutes, I will be feeling warm and gooey inside, having lots of loving feelings for him and grateful to be married to the best man in the world. Nothing in my marriage has changed. The circumstances and issues are exactly what they were minutes ago. My current state of being has little to do with anything my husband did or did not do or the reality of the present state of our marriage. Reality is not a factor here. What dictates my reality and my experience is how I think on it.

A man is what he thinks about all day long.

Ralph Waldo Emerson

It is just like a Polaroid camera. You aim, focus and within seconds, your photo develops. It is the same with us. What we focus on is what develops.

It is all in how you see it. There is power in perspective, and the good news is we have the power to change our perspective.

We can complain because rose bushes have thorns, or rejoice because thorn bushes have roses.

Abraham Lincoln

God gave us free will. He tells us to think on what is praiseworthy, and we want to think on thoughts that are good, but why is it so hard? Have you noticed that it almost seems more natural and normal to think about what is wrong instead of what is right? Why is that? Why does the natural flow of an unchecked mind seem to go straight to the gutter and think on every single negative thing imaginable?

I read a magazine interview with Sharon Stone in which she was quoted as saying, "Someone once told me I have a mind like a bad neighborhood; I shouldn't go in there alone." Ha!

I can relate. I think we can all relate. So can Eve, because this dynamic goes all the way back to the Garden. In the book of Genesis, the Lord told Eve she could eat from any tree in the Garden. As far as her eyes could see, everything before her was hers for the taking. She could have it all and eat from it all except for one tree. One tree was forbidden. So, did Eve think about all the trees in the Garden that she could eat from and all the delicious fruit available to her? Nope, all she could think of was that one tree that she couldn't have. Just like Eve, our mind does not naturally gravitate toward all we have, but to what we do not have.

Our mind, left to its own devices, will always think on what is negative, what is missing, what is lacking. We must purposefully fix our minds on what is good, what is lovely and what is praiseworthy (see Philippians 4:8–9). It does not happen naturally; it is a choice of the will.

I have set before you life and death, blessing and cursing; therefore choose life, that both you and your descendants may live.

Deuteronomy 30:19

One way to choose life is to think thoughts that bring life. How we think and what we think shapes who we become.

For as [a man] thinks in his heart, so is he.

Proverbs 23:7

For many of us, our minds have been contaminated for years with an abundance of clutter that is not from God. Imagine your mind as a glass of water full of dirt particles. You would not attempt to purify the water by picking each particle of dirt out with your fingers. That would be an arduous and ineffective task, to say the least. The most effortless way to achieve a clear glass of water is to continue to pour fresh water into the glass until the dirt is flushed up and out and all that remains is pure water. The process of renewing our mind is much the same. By replacing wrong thoughts with God thoughts, we are washing our mind with the pure water of the Word until all the junky thoughts are flushed out (see Ephesians 5:26).

Begin to practice purposeful thinking. Pick a Scripture about the goodness of God, and meditate on it. Spend a minute or two thinking about how something important to you, such as your marriage or your relationship with the Lord, would look in an ideal scenario, and ruminate on it. On purpose, put your mind somewhere praiseworthy or on something you are believing God for even if reality doesn't line up with the facts yet. Remember, it is not the circumstances in life that bring peace and joy, but how we choose to think about the circumstances that determine our emotional state and our reality. What we think about shapes what we believe and forms the truth from which we live.

Contrary to popular, secular belief, truth is not subjective. It is not "whatever feels right to me is my truth, and whatever feels right to you is your truth." There is no "my truth" and "your truth." There is *the* truth, one ultimate truth, and that is the truth of the Word of God, period. Therefore, if we want to partake in the promises and blessings available to us as Christians, then it is our job to align our personal truth with *the* truth of the Bible. We do that by recognizing where our thoughts do not agree with the Word and purposefully replacing them.

Recognizing and replacing thoughts is like a muscle that strengthens with practice over time. At first, you might not catch your negative thinking until you have spent a solid hour fretting and worrying. But once you start practicing, you can shorten the time. It might be thirty minutes and the next time five minutes. Soon you will become adept at identifying and shifting your mind and you will be able to catch thoughts at the onset. That is when life begins to change, and you find yourself in a lot more peace throughout your day. And not only does your internal world shift by taking thoughts captive, but your external world begins to shift as well. Holding fast to the Word of God and the truths therein, not allowing our minds to waver, causes our circumstances to shift out of their current factual realm and begin to line up with the truth of God's Word. That is faith in action. In the natural realm the expression is "I have to see it to believe it." In the Kingdom it is the opposite: We have to believe it in order to see it. For something to manifest and become a reality, we first have to believe it.

19

The Sword

For the word of God is living and powerful,
and sharper than any two-edged sword.

Hebrews 4:12

Our first God-given tool for transformation is our mind. How we think and what we think shapes who we become. Our second tool for transformation carries with it the ability to destroy or build up. It can be used as a mighty weapon of warfare imbued with the power to slay our adversary or as a conduit to appropriate God's blessings into our lives. This tool, also built into our bodies and ready to be activated at our command, is our mouth.

The words we speak out of our own mouths have more power than we know. James chapter one says if we ask for wisdom our Father will give it to us liberally (v. 5). In asking for wisdom and understanding regarding the power of the mouth, I was led by the Holy Spirit to read the book of wisdom: Proverbs. From the beginning of the book to the end, I was astounded at how many Scriptures address the mouth, so much that I decided to study the subject more thoroughly. Using a concordance, I looked up every verse in Proverbs that included the words *mouth, lips* and *tongue*. Amazingly, there are almost a hundred such Scriptures just in the book of Proverbs alone! I encourage all believers to do a study of their own on the mouth and put together a compilation of Scriptures, but here are a few from Proverbs that resonated strongly with me (emphasis mine):

You are snared by the words of your **mouth**; you are taken by the words of your **mouth**.

Proverbs 6:2

Listen, for I will speak of excellent things, and from the opening of my **lips** will come right things.

Proverbs 8:6

Wise people store up knowledge, but the **mouth** of the foolish is near destruction.

Proverbs 10:14

In the multitude of words sin is not lacking, but he who restrains his **lips** is wise.

Proverbs 10:19

The **tongue** of the righteous is choice silver.

Proverbs 10:20

He who guards his **mouth** preserves his life, but he who opens wide his **lips** shall have destruction.

Proverbs 13:3

A wholesome **tongue** is a tree of life, but perverseness in it breaks the spirit.

Proverbs 15:4

She opens her **mouth** with wisdom, and on her **tongue** is the law of kindness.

Proverbs 31:26

And one of my personal favorites that includes all three words: mouth, lips and tongue:

A man's stomach shall be satisfied from the fruit of his **mouth**; from the produce of his **lips** he shall be filled. Death and life are in the power of the **tongue**, and those who love it will eat its fruit.

Proverbs 18:20–21

Death and life are in the power of the tongue. Wow! That is an eye-opener and hopefully a mouth closer! Talk about life-changing revelation. What we speak affects our lives *every* day and in *every* way—and most of us have little awareness of the degree in which our words shape our lives.

Prospering in every area, including our health, is a direct result of how we prosper in our soul, which is our mind, will and emotions.

Beloved, I pray that you may prosper in all things and be in health, just as your soul prospers.

3 John 2

And one of the determining factors of our soul prospering is how we speak! According to Scripture, what we say can either be a snare to our soul or keep our soul from troubles.

A fool's mouth is his destruction, and his lips are the snare of his soul.

Proverbs 18:7

Whoever guards his mouth and tongue keeps his soul from troubles.

Proverbs 21:23

And here are two proverbs that confirm the tremendous effect of our words in regard to our health.

There is one who speaks like the piercings of a sword, but the tongue of the wise promotes health.

Proverbs 12:18

The heart of the wise teaches his mouth, and adds learning to his lips. Pleasant words *are like* a honeycomb, sweetness to the soul and health to the bones.

Proverbs 16:23–24

So to sum up, Scripture teaches that a vital aspect of our physical and emotional well-being is determined, not so much by our circumstances, but by *what we say* about our circumstances. Our tongue wields more power than we know. You might have heard the saying, "The pen is mightier than the sword." Well, the mouth can also be mightier than the sword. As a matter of fact, it is our sword.

Finally, my brethren, be strong in the Lord and in the power of His might. Put on the whole armor of God, that you may be able to stand against the wiles of the devil. For we do not wrestle against flesh and blood, but against principalities, against powers, against the rulers of the darkness of this age, against spiritual hosts of wickedness in the heavenly places.

Therefore take up the whole armor of God, that you may be able to withstand in the evil day, and having done all, to stand. Stand therefore, having girded your waist with truth, having put on the breastplate of righteousness, and having shod your feet with the preparation of the gospel of peace; above all, taking the shield of faith with which you will be able to quench all the fiery darts of the wicked one. And take the helmet of salvation, and the sword of the Spirit, which is the word of God.

Ephesians 6:10–17

Notice that almost every piece of armor we have been given is for defense and worn as protection. We have only been given one offensive piece of armor, a weapon with which to fight, and that is the sword, the Word of God. It is no coincidence that the root word of SWORD is WORD. The Word we speak out loud is our weapon for warfare. It is our sword. How do we use this sword of the Word during spiritual warfare? Jesus modeled it for us in Luke 4:

Then Jesus, being filled with the Holy Spirit, returned from the Jordan and was led by the Spirit into the wilderness, being tempted for forty days by the devil. And in those days He ate nothing, and afterward, when they had ended, He was hungry. And the devil said to Him, "If You are the Son of God, command this stone to become bread." But Jesus answered him, saying, "It is written, 'Man shall not live by bread alone, but by every word of God.'" Then the devil, taking Him up on a high mountain, showed Him all the kingdoms of the world in a moment of time. And the devil said to Him, "All this authority I will give You, and their glory; for this has been delivered to me, and I give it to whomever I wish. Therefore, if You will worship before me, all will be Yours." And Jesus answered and said to him, "Get behind Me, Satan! For it is written, 'You shall worship the LORD your God, and Him only you shall serve.'" Then he brought Him to Jerusalem, set Him on the pinnacle of the temple, and said to Him, "If You are the Son of God, throw Yourself down from here. For it is written: 'He shall give His angels charge over you, to keep you,' and, 'In their hands they shall bear you up, lest you dash your foot against a stone.'" And Jesus answered and said to him, "It has been said, 'You shall not tempt the LORD your God.'" Now when the devil had ended every temptation, he departed from Him until an opportune time.

Luke 4:1–13

Each time Satan came at Jesus with lies and tried to tempt Him, Jesus replied with the truth of the Word. Jesus fought with the sword of the Spirit, speaking the Word of God, and we must fight the same way. When we are bombarded in our mind with lies from the enemy, we must take those thoughts captive and purposefully set our mind on what is true.

For the weapons of our warfare are not carnal but mighty in God for pulling down strongholds, casting down arguments and every high thing that exalts itself against the knowledge of God, bringing every thought into captivity to the obedience of Christ.

2 Corinthians 10:4–5

Finally, brethren, whatever things are true, whatever things are noble, whatever things are just, whatever things are pure, whatever things are lovely, whatever things are of good report, if there is any virtue and if there is anything praiseworthy—meditate on these things. The things which you learned and received and heard and saw in me, these do, and the God of peace will be with you.

Philippians 4:8–9

Understanding the power of words is the first step. The next action is to pick up our sword and use it.

Using the Sword

We use our sword by not only thinking what is true, but by speaking what is true out of our mouths. We use our sword of the Spirit by speaking out loud. Speaking the Word out loud automatically shifts our thinking. If our mind is spinning with thoughts that we cannot seem to stop, then speaking contrary thoughts—those that line up with the truth of the Word—helps to halt the mind and forces it to switch gears. It is almost impossible to be speaking one thing and thinking another simultaneously. Let us look at a few benefits of speaking the Word of God.

Speaking the Word Strengthens Faith and Belief in the Word

Faith comes by hearing, and hearing by the word of God.

Romans 10:17

We are usually taught this Scripture to encourage us to go to church and hear the Word so that our faith will be strengthened. That is true, but there is another aspect to this Scripture. What we hear our own selves say has just as much, if not more, influence over our lives than what we hear others say to us; therefore, when we hear the Word coming out of our own mouth, it has a tremendous impact in increasing our faith. Many of us pray to have greater faith, and we long to believe everything that the Word of God says, but there are areas where we struggle to believe. There have been many times that I prayed and pleaded like this verse:

"Lord, . . . help my unbelief!"

Mark 9:24

We want to believe, and we try to believe, but how do we get to the place where we truly believe deep down? In addition to praying, there is a way we can change what we believe in our hearts, and that is by speaking what we want to believe out of our mouth.

Our words affect what we believe.

According to Scripture, what we speak about reveals what is in our hearts.

For out of the abundance of the heart his mouth speaks.

Luke 6:45

Our words do reveal what we believe, *but* our words also go back into our hearts and are like seeds that we sow into ourselves that play a huge part in forming and shaping what we believe. This is the spiritual principle of *what you sow will grow*. We know this is true regarding finances, but it applies to every area of our lives. If we speak and sow words of faith, then our faith grows. If we speak and sow words of unbelief, then that is what will reside within our hearts.

Here is another piece to ponder: If we want to find out what we really believe in our hearts, we should pay attention to our words. Our words reveal our hearts and will tell us if we are in faith or unbelief. Once we listen to our own words we are able to determine what we truly believe and then we can choose to change what we believe by sowing different words into our hearts. One of the ways we change what we believe is by speaking what is true according to the Word regardless of the facts.

In some ways the mind is like a computer. A computer does not evaluate whether its data is true or not. It merely receives what is imputed. As we "reprogram" the computer of our mind with the truth of the Word over the fact of our circumstances, eventually that truth becomes dominant in our mind and heart. This is part of the how-to process of renewing our mind.

Speaking the Word Renews the Mind

Scripture says that we can have the mind of Christ (see 1 Corinthians 2:16), meaning we can think as Christ thinks, once we are renewed in the spirit of our mind.

> . . . Be renewed in the spirit of your mind, and that you put on the new man which was created according to God, in true righteousness and holiness.
>
> Ephesians 4:23–24

To *renew* means "to replace," so as we replace lies with truth, and then speak those truths out loud, we are literally in the act of transforming our minds to the mind of Christ and putting on the new man. Speaking the Word of God purifies our mind, and it is one of the ways that we are sanctified and cleansed "with the washing of water by the word" (Ephesians 5:26).

Speaking the Word Alters the Spiritual and Natural Realm

Just as Jesus modeled in Luke chapter four, the Word of God spoken out loud is a weapon used to fight the adversary. As we just recognized from the multiple Scriptures in Proverbs, what we speak has a great effect on both our physical body and our soul.

Think of it this way: When we speak, it is as if our words are carried in wet cement. They are malleable as they flow from our mouth, but as our words land, the cement dries and those spoken words become anchored into our lives. What is spoken becomes cemented into reality, and in many ways, becomes our reality.

Change your words, change your life.

For we all stumble in many things. If anyone does not stumble
in word, he is a perfect man, able also to bridle the whole body.
Indeed, we put bits in horses' mouths that they may obey us,
and we turn their whole body. Look also at ships: although they
are so large and are driven by fierce winds, they are turned by
a very small rudder wherever the pilot desires.

James 3:2–4

Read that again: "If anyone doesn't stumble in word, he is a
perfect man." *Perfect* in this Scripture means "to be mature." It
is not about trying to be perfect before God, meaning making
no mistakes; it is about the maturity of being able to rein in
the tongue. This passage goes on to say that if you are able to
bridle the tongue, you are, in turn, able to bridle your entire
body. There is a correlation between where the tongue goes
and where the body goes. Actually, the tongue drives the body
in the way it goes. This Scripture in James explains that just as
a bit in a horse's mouth steers the horse, and as a rudder on a
ship turns a ship, our tongues literally direct our bodies and
the course of our lives.

That is no small statement. In light of this truth, ask yourself,
How many words do I speak that are directing the course of my life?
The answer: All of them. Then ponder this: *How many words
do I speak that agree with the Word of God and direct the course of
my life in the way in which I, and God, want it to go?* When I first
began to learn about this principle, sadly, my own answer was:
not many.

Just as we have spent time pondering what we are *thinking*
about, now it is time to think about what we are *talking* about.
Do you speak any of the following phrases over your life on
a regular basis?:

- *I'm so tired.*
- *I can't even look at a cookie without gaining five pounds.*
- *It's Murphy's Law, if something bad is going to happen, you had better believe it's going to happen to me.*
- *I'm just sick and tired.*
- *I can't take it anymore.*
- *My mind is not what it used to be. I can't remember a thing.*
- *I'm getting old. Nothing is working like it used to.*
- *My body is falling apart.*

Keep in mind that what we say in jest or sarcastically still has power. Just because it might be a joke, does not make it exempt from carrying weight. And while some of the above statements may be factual, the last thing we want to do is cement them as truth in our lives. Yeah, you might be tired, but you do not need to tell thirty people about it. You might not be feeling great but you do not have to proclaim it all day long. All that does is establish those circumstances and root them into your life. We want to speak fewer facts that are negative and more words of truth that are full of life.

Try an experiment. Take a week or so and pay attention to the conversations of others. Eavesdrop at the gym or while standing in line at the grocery store checkout. Notice how common it is in our society to connect with one another through reporting ailments and negative circumstances. You will probably hear a lot of conversations that go something like this:

Person A asks, "How are you?"

Person B answers, "Horrible. My back is killing me. I had a car accident five years ago; the doctors told me it is only going to get worse. When the weather is like this, forget about it." And they usually continue on and on relaying every ailment and negative detail ever spoken about their health.

Person A often jumps on board the negativity train here because as the saying goes: Misery loves company. "Your back hurts? Let me tell you about my shoulder." They proceed with going back and forth in an effort to one-up each other and see who will come out the victor in the game of who has it worse. After fifteen minutes of doom and gloom "bonding" and rooting all the negative circumstances deeply into their realities, they conclude by saying: "So great seeing you and catching up. Have a good day." Really? This is truly impossible now that all the negative talking has directed the thoughts and emotions more deeply into the negative.

Just recently I was with my daughter who was playing at the park. Within five minutes of striking up a conversation with another mom, she told me how fearful she was about possible child molesters in the neighborhood. She went on to say that she wanted to have more kids but figured she was too old; all her eggs had dried up. Before walking away, she threw in a couple more self-deprecating comments about her capacity to think straight and her body type, then bid me farewell. Oh dear! And this was a casual, five-minute conversation with a complete stranger! It saddens me that this is how we socialize with one another: speaking death over our families, our lives and ourselves.

When it comes to a question like "How are you?" we need to teach ourselves how to answer!

> The heart of the wise teaches his mouth, and adds learning to his lips.
>
> Proverbs 16:23

The wise teaches his mouth. I love that. I have to teach my mouth what to say because it is not going to go to the positive naturally. The mouth has a mind of its own, and just like the mind, the mouth wants to go south. It likes to gossip, fault find, complain and be downright negative. Therefore, I must teach my mouth how to speak. I have to train it to agree with the truth of the Word and speak what is good and what is praiseworthy (see Philippians 4).

Now add this to your experiment: Listen to yourself as you chat with friends and co-workers. Make a mental note of the kinds of subjects you gravitate toward discussing, and see if you can practice socializing without reporting any negative information. Do not say one negative thing about anything! This might come as a shock to your system as you recognize that you have no idea how to communicate without being negative. If that is the case, you might choose to be a little quieter than usual. Ask questions and practice listening more and talking less while you are learning. Less talking can be a good thing as you retrain yourself how to speak.

> So then, my beloved brethren, let every man be swift to hear, slow to speak, slow to wrath.
>
> James 1:19

That is the exact opposite for most of us. We are usually very quick to speak and slow to listen! We are quick in sharing every thought and feeling and circumstance, not realizing that the more we talk, the easier it is to get into trouble with doom and gloom talking.

> In the multitude of words sin is not lacking, but he who restrains his lips is wise.
>
> Proverbs 10:19

Does that mean we are not to talk? No, it is merely the wisdom of the Word of God instructing us. Just as the natural person thinks upon whatever enters the mind but the spiritual person disciplines his mind and takes his thoughts captive, the natural person says whatever he feels or thinks. He speaks loosely and freely with little restraint, but spiritual persons guard their mouths and choose their words carefully knowing that death and life are in the power of the tongue (see Proverbs 18:21).

So, death or life is not a result of what happens to me, but dependent on what I speak in regard to what happens to me. Powerful! Scripture teaches us that death or life is a choice. It is a buffet laid out before us daily, and we choose from which we will eat.

> I have set before you life and death, blessing and cursing; therefore choose life, that both you and your descendants may live.
>
> Deuteronomy 30:19

How do we choose life? One way is by speaking life. Do you want your life to change drastically and radically? Make a decision to refuse to allow anything negative to come out of your mouth. Adopt this mindset: I will not give voice to what *is* according to my senses—what I see and what I feel—but I will declare what *is to come* according to God's plans and purposes for my life. Instead of continuing to speak about the struggles, and the dry and dead places in my life, I will model Abraham in Romans 4:17 and speak as "God, who gives life to the dead and calls those things which do not exist as though they did." I choose to speak life!

20

Choose Life—Speak Life

To speak and to speak well are two different
things. A fool may talk, but a wise man speaks.

Ben Jonson

Some of my darkest days in dealing with issues, food especially, were after I had become a Christian. Once I was adopted into God's kingdom, the adversary turned up the heat to take me out of my calling, my purpose and my destiny. The enemy was not playing around. He was targeting me with the sole intent to steal, kill and destroy. I decided to get serious. I would no longer take a solely defensive stance in my walk, but instead, I began to assume an offensive position. I decided to pointedly go after the enemy with the same intensity that he was going after me.

I have pursued my enemies and overtaken them; neither did
I turn back again till they were destroyed.

Psalm 18:37

One definition of pursue is "to follow in order to overtake, capture, kill or defeat." This verse in Psalm 18 enforces that as long as I stick with it and do not give up, I can and will defeat the enemy, that I can and will get free. The enemy will not overtake me, but with effort, I will overtake him. A part of my strategy against him was to recognize my weak places, the places where I was most vulnerable to his attack.

> Therefore strengthen the hands which hang down, and the feeble knees, and make straight paths for your feet, so that what is lame may not be dislocated, but rather be healed.
>
> Hebrews 12:12–13

Upon learning that scriptural truth, I purposefully began to strengthen my "feeble" and "lame" places by using the sword of the Spirit, which is the Word of God. I decided to wage war on the enemy and fight for my life. I bought a notebook, and I began to write down every area in which I was struggling. I penned every lie the enemy fed me in an effort to dominate my thinking. Then I spent a good deal of time studying the Bible and finding Scriptures to combat those lies. This was back in the day, prior to owning a PC, so I sat on my living room floor with a concordance and five Bibles in various translations. It is much easier now with online Bible websites where you can type in any word, such as *faith,* and every verse that contains the word *faith* comes up in an organized list in any translation you choose. I am grateful for technology. It does make studying more efficient and less time consuming, but there is something about my old school approach that I would not trade for anything. I had to dig deep to find answers, and dig I did!

I began examining my handwritten list of lies: anxiety, worry, self-doubt, self-hatred, fear, financial pressure and a skewed perception of my body and myself, to name a few. I started at the top of my list with anxiety. After looking up the words *anxious* and *anxiety* in my concordance, I launched into a study session, thoroughly examining everything the Bible had to say on the topic. As I read through each Scripture, I wrote down the ones that especially resonated with me—those that felt right on target with what I was going through and spoke directly to my heart. I continued down my list of lies, finding correlating Scriptures to combat each and every one. Days later, I had a notebook filled with page after page of Scriptures. My sword was ready to go!

My first strike of the sword was reading through my list, out loud, on a regular basis. Sometimes I would read the entire list of Scriptures, and at other times, I would focus on one specific category. I did this knowing that I was planting the Word like a seed believing that, in time, those seeds would bear fruit. I also decided, for the areas I was most challenged in, to memorize Scripture. Then, when I was out and about, I could pull those Scriptures out of my arsenal to fight in the moment they were needed.

I encourage you to get a notebook and do a study of your own. Load your tool belt with Scripture to fight your fight. Invest the time that it takes. You are worth it. The more time you invest, the stronger and more apt with the sword you will become. The words that we speak that are in alignment with the Word of God will always produce good fruit in our lives. In other words, the Word works.

Personalizing the Word

I'll start you off with a small excerpt from my personal repertoire. I always speak my Scriptures in first person and suggest you do the same. You want to personalize it; it is more powerful when you do. You own it. I also like to paraphrase certain Scriptures to make them more conversational. As you read the following section of Scripture, read each verse out loud, and see how it feels to have the Word of God flowing out of your mouth.

Anxiety:

I am anxious for nothing, but in everything by prayer and supplication, with thanksgiving, I let my requests be made known to God; and the peace of God, which passes all understanding, guards my heart and mind through Christ Jesus.

See Philippians 4:6–7

Worry:

I do not worry about my life, what I will eat, what I will drink or about my body; what I will put on. . . . [My God knows what I need] so I seek first the kingdom of God and His righteousness, and all those things shall be added unto me.

See Matthew 6:25, 6:33

Finances:

My God shall supply all my need according to His riches in glory by Christ Jesus.

See Philippians 4:19

Abandonment and Rejection:

My father and my mother might have forsaken me, but the LORD will take care of me.

See Psalm 27:10

He will never leave me or forsake me. The LORD is my helper; I will not fear. What can man do to me?

See Hebrews 13:5–6

Self-Hatred:

I will praise You for I am fearfully and wonderfully made.

See Psalm 139:14

Condemnation:

There is therefore now no condemnation to those who are in Christ Jesus, who do not walk according to the flesh, but according to the Spirit. I am in Christ, therefore there is no condemnation toward me.

See Romans 8:1

Weariness:

I will not grow weary while doing good, because I know that in due season I will reap if I do not lose heart.

See Galatians 6:9

Weakness:

I can do all things through Christ who strengthens me.

See Philippians 4:13

I am strong in the Lord and in the power of His might.

See Ephesians 6:10

Self-Worth:

I am a chosen generation, a royal priesthood, a holy nation, His own special person, that I may proclaim the praises of Him who called me out of darkness into His marvelous light.

See 1 Peter 2:9

Hopelessness:

The Lord's thoughts toward me are of peace and not of evil. He will give me a future and a hope.

See Jeremiah 29:11

Torment:

I have the mind of Christ.

See 1 Corinthians 2:16

Peace:

I have perfect peace because my mind is stayed on Him, and I trust in Him.

See Isaiah 26:3

Trust:

I trust in the LORD with all my heart, and lean not on my own understanding; in all my ways I acknowledge Him, and He shall direct my paths.

See Proverbs 3:5–6

In God I have put my trust; I will not be afraid. What can man do to me?

See Psalm 56:11

Forgiveness and Offense:

I am quick to forgive.

See Colossians 3:13 MSG

I keep no record of wrongs.

See 1 Corinthians 13:5 NLT

190

Because my greatest passion is for freedom from torment, addictions, fear and everything else I felt controlled by, here are some of my heavy hitters that were in constant rotation:

Freedom:

I am free, for whom the Son sets free is free indeed.

See John 8:36

Where the Spirit of the Lord is, there is liberty.

2 Corinthians 3:17

When I felt an overwhelming desire to binge, I would say this next one almost as if I were pointing my finger directly at the enemy and commanding him through this Scripture to "Back off!" It was a declaration that it is the Lord who sustains me—not food. I refused to allow my destiny to be stolen from me.

Food and Binge Eating:

I have food to eat of which you do not know. My food is to do the will of Him who sent me and finish His work.

See John 4:32, 34

And I just about wore out my sword with this last Scripture!

Fear:

God has not given me a spirit of fear, but of power, and of love, and of a sound mind.

See 2 Timothy 1:7

There were days when I would be driving in my car and feel the fear swoop in, and I would declare this Scripture about fear over and over—maybe fifty times. I remember hearing this thought in my head (the enemy of course), "Hi, crazy person.

Look at yourself, driving around saying a sentence over and over again. Do you really think this is doing anything?" I knew then, just because of that thought, that the repetition of that Scripture was making an indelible impression. Otherwise, the enemy would not be working so diligently to coerce me to stop.

I responded out loud, just as Jesus did in Luke chapter four, "I don't care if I look crazy. The Word of God works, and I'm going to say it a thousand times if that's what it takes. You are not going to stop me!" Interestingly enough, that was the last time the enemy hit me with that dart. Funny how the enemy backs off when we take a stand in the Spirit.

I made a decision that day: I did not care how long it would take. I was determined to speak the Word of God until I saw change. Even if I did not see results right away, I chose to believe that the Word was true; and in time, my life would mirror what I was speaking. My tenacity paid off. After years of planting seeds and using my sword, I am no longer racked with fear the way I used to be. I am no longer tormented every second about my weight and my body. I literally do not deal with any of that anymore, but it did not happen overnight. I had to fight for that territory—fight until I got it. Now I am living within the freedom I so desperately and diligently sought. So for you, instead of just reading and hearing these Scriptures, they can become a reality in your life as well. Be unwavering. Resolve to do whatever it takes for as long as it takes to get free. God gives us a choice as to how we want to live. Here He says,

"I call heaven and earth as witnesses today against you, that I have set before you life and death, blessing and cursing; therefore choose life, that both you and your descendants may live."

Deuteronomy 30:19

Notice how the Lord is not saying, "If you are a Christian, and if you love Me, you will have life." No, He is saying *choose*

192

life. Our Father supplies us with everything we need through His Word, but we must *choose* to use the tools and adhere to the biblical principles He has put in place in order to be successful. It is what we choose that elicits change or stagnation, life or death.

Speaking life, the term I use to mean "to speak the Word of God out loud," is not an attempt to control people or manipulate God. That would be witchcraft, because manipulation in any form is witchcraft. Speaking life is also not "name it and claim it," where we choose worldly things we want and expect God to do what we say. It is not taking the Word and perverting it for selfish gain like, "I want a Porsche, and I declare it so." Speaking life is not about fulfilling the soul's desires at all. It is much deeper than that. When we speak out the Word, we say the same thing God says. This becomes an effective tool to renew our minds (see Romans 12:2) and to plant the Word in our hearts. Speaking life means agreeing with the truth of the Word over the fact of our circumstances as Paul reminded us to do when he said, "We also believe and therefore speak" (2 Corinthians 4:13). It also reinforces the belief in our hearts as we fight the good fight of faith (see 1 Timothy 6:12). In essence, we are aligning our words with the Word of God, which positions us to receive the promises that are ours in Christ.

Speaking life is not using our words to get what we want. It is using our words to align ourselves with what God has already given us. Just as we train ourselves to practice purposeful thinking by concentrating on what brings life, speaking life is purposeful speaking. You can believe God for any area of your life where you want to grow, heal or prosper, and you back up your belief and put it into action by speaking. Do you want more joy? Speak Scriptures about joy. Are you being challenged in your finances? Find every Scripture on finances and begin to proclaim them. Do you long for greater spiritual revelation and discernment? Go to Ephesians 1:17–19 and personalize the words by declaring,

> "I thank You, Lord, for the spirit of wisdom and revelation in the knowledge of You, that the eyes of my understanding would be enlightened; that I may know what is the hope of Your calling, what are the riches of the glory of Your inheritance in the saints, and what is the exceeding greatness of Your power toward me who believes."

We can speak life in the moment of spiritual warfare by using our sword to slay the enemy, or we can use the sword of the Word to plant the truth into our hearts and minds anytime we choose. The Word we sow is seed that will spring forth and produce fruit. The more seed we sow the greater the harvest until we become a living manifestation of the truth of the Word of God.

> We are what we repeatedly do. Excellence then, is not an act, but a habit.
>
> Aristotle

With all due respect to Aristotle, allow me to embellish from a Christian perspective: We become what we repeatedly do, think and say. The more we do, think and say the truth of what God says, the more we transform and become who we were originally created to be. Amen!

21

Don't Give Up

Although the world is full of suffering,
it is full also of overcoming.

Helen Keller

Everyone suffers. It is an inevitable part of life on earth. But the difference for believers is that when we stay connected to God we have Someone to help us. Instead of our suffering overtaking us to the point where we cannot go on, we have a Person who walks through the fire alongside us. He will lift our sorrows and carry our burdens, so we are able to keep moving forward with our loads lightened. Jesus said,

"Come to Me, all you who labor and are heavy laden, and I will give you rest. Take My yoke upon you and learn from Me, for I am gentle and lowly in heart, and you will find rest for your souls. For My yoke is easy and My burden is light."

Matthew 11:28–30

The Lord *asks* us to come to Him so He can remove every weight. When we have been through a lot and have had to endure for a long time, it is easy to give up hope. The last thing you want to do is open your heart again and set yourself up for more disappointment. However, we have to make a decision to believe that with this newfound understanding, and with practical tools for transformation, things can and will change.

Renewed hope is a catalyst for change.

Hope deferred makes the heart sick, but when the desire comes, it is a tree of life.

Proverbs 13:12

Hopelessness is death; hope is life. Allowing yourself to hope again sparks a flame that propels you toward life and all that you have yearned for your life to be. Be willing to risk; dare to dream.

Most of the important things in the world have been accomplished by people who have kept on trying when there seemed to be no hope at all.

Dale Carnegie

Optimism is the faith that leads to achievement. Nothing can be done without hope and confidence.

Helen Keller

Even if I knew that tomorrow the world would go to pieces, I would still plant my apple tree.

Martin Luther

Hope is essential, along with a good dose of tenacity. Even when there seems to be no hope at all, we must choose to hope and choose to persist. We have talked a lot about choice and decisions of the will. It is imperative to assume an inner attitude of the heart that says, "I don't care how it looks around me. Nothing is going to stop me from hoping, dreaming and believing." We must determine to be like Abraham, who did not waver at the promise of God through unbelief, but was strengthened in faith, giving glory to God, and was fully convinced that what He had promised, He was also able to perform (see Romans 4:20–21). Let that truth squelch any thoughts of *But I hoped and got nowhere. I've tried and I've failed. I've fallen short; I'm scared to try again.* Falling and "failing" are common characteristics of the process on your way to success. When a baby learns to walk they fall often. None of us would consider those falls failures. Our growth is contingent upon viewing our progress through a lens of gentleness and compassion. In the process of moving forward we step, we slip, and at times, we stop moving completely. We even go in the wrong direction or fall off the path. That is not failure but an ordained part of the journey.

For a righteous man may fall seven times and rise again.

Proverbs 24:16

A righteous man may fall seven times, but the good news is that God provides grace for all of our falls. I wish I had only fallen seven times or blown it seven times! I have messed up many more times than that, but it is not about how many times we blow it—it is about how many times we get back up. It is about the oomph to keep going, and that oomph has to trump the voice that says, "It's never going to happen for me."

Are you dead yet? If there is breath in your body, then God is fashioning your future.

For I know the thoughts that I think toward you, says the LORD, thoughts of peace and not of evil, to give you a future and a hope.

Jeremiah 29:11

And let us not grow weary while doing good, for in due season we shall reap if we do not lose heart.

Galatians 6:9

What a statement in Galatians! This verse is a promise from God. We will reap if we stay in faith and keep hoping and believing. Our adversary does not steal our promises as much as he steals our hope and faith as we wait for them to unfold. He knows the only way he can thwart what God has for us is to persuade us to quit. He works diligently at manipulating us into feeling defeated because he knows if we stay the course we *will* receive what God has planned for us.

It is God's job for me to reap.
It is my job to keep hope alive and not lose heart.

When we get hit with thoughts and feelings urging us to give up, we have to recognize it as warfare, resist it with everything we've got, and hold fast to the truth that we will reap in due season. The "in due season" part is the challenge. You might think, *I can't do this one more day.* We have all felt that way. There were numerous times as a Christian when I felt like I could not do this whole God thing for one more minute. My heart cried out, *Why is it so hard? Why is it so long? When is my "due season" going to get here already?* There were multiple times when I wanted to throw in the towel and declare, "I'm done."

One day I was in that "I'm done" place and felt the Holy Spirit unction my spirit, saying, *Really, where are you going to go?* That made me laugh. He continued, *With all you know in*

198

the Lord, and all you have experienced, do you really think you could walk away? There is no way you could live denying truth. You would last about a minute.

It's true; life is hard. It is hard even with God, but without Him? I do not know how people do it. With the Lord, *nothing* we go through is for naught. He will use all of our trials to prosper us as long as we continue pressing into Him. Stay the course and . . .

**Your test will become your testimony,
and your mess will become your message.**

For years I was consumed with my body, my weight and every morsel of food that went into my mouth. I was fearful, mentally tormented and in a perpetual state of emotional discomfort. I had no peace. Now all of that incessant torment is gone; I do not live there anymore. Did my healing happen in a few months? No, it took longer than that, but in staying close to the Lord and putting these tools into practice, eventually the change did come. What had been disastrous in my life is now my message. What had almost pushed me to the brink has become my testimony of how I overcame and how you can, too.

Feel your feelings, stop, drop and roll, get on-the-floor, cast your cares, identify thoughts, take them captive, use your sword and speak the Word . . . phew! Seems like a lot of work! It is. Everything worth having takes some work, but I do not mind working if my work produces results. One thing I know for sure is God's ways produce results! Most of us are frustrated and worn out from trying so hard, and because we have been using the wrong tools for the job for so long. A different kind of effort is required when you are working with the proper tools. Taking thoughts captive, identifying lies and replacing them with the truth can feel like a full-time job at first. For a season you might find yourself working these tools endlessly.

Do not allow that to concern or derail you. It takes persistence and concentrated effort, but once you gain ground, a new pattern will emerge, and in time you will find you no longer need to focus on certain areas with such intensity. You will just be different.

> As a single footstep will not make a path on the earth, so a single thought will not make a pathway in the mind. To make a deep physical path, we walk again and again. To make a deep mental path, we must think over and over the kind of thoughts we wish to dominate our lives.
>
> Henry David Thoreau

Think of your mind like a flowing river kept intact by rocks along the riverbed. Imagine trying to alter the course of the river. We cannot lift up a body of water, but we can redirect its course by moving the rocks one by one that line the riverbed. In time a new course is charted and the river has a new path. It is the same process for our mind and life. Each time we stop, drop and roll, we are moving a rock. Each time we take a thought captive and replace it with a God thought, we are moving a rock. Each time we use our sword and speak life, we are moving a rock. For a season you will be spending a lot of time moving rocks, but in time you will be able to rest and enjoy the fruit of your labor. Your mind will naturally flow in a different way, and you will find you no longer think like you used to think or feel how you used to feel. You will no longer be in bondage to what used to enslave you.

We change our thinking and our lives one rock at a time.

Our natural inclination with this new information is to strive to make it happen faster. You might be thinking, *One rock at a time is pretty slow. Let's get this thing moving. Let's get this river streaming in a new direction already.* The temptation is to start picking up as many rocks as you can possibly hold in an attempt to move your entire riverbed at once. Before you know it you will be weighed down, overwhelmed and find yourself lying under a huge rock pile unable to move. This is how you wear yourself out. Resist the urge to do too much. Take a breath, and recognize that this is a process and it will take time. Gently and easily move one rock at a time. There is no pressure. Move a rock and then stand back and rest awhile. Take your hands off of how quickly or slowly the change is happening, and allow it to unfold. You might be thinking, *But I've already lost so much time. I could've/should've been there by now. I'm so old.* First of all, you are exactly where you are supposed to be. Second, God is supernatural, and He can restore time to us. One of God's favorite ways to work is in the manner of "a suddenly." Perhaps it appears that you are at a standstill, not moving forward at all, just like the caterpillar in the cocoon. It seems like nothing is happening—zero, zilch, nada. Then all of a sudden one day—*BAM*—you are a butterfly. It can be days, weeks and months of nothing, nothing, nothing, and then out of nowhere, in the blink of an eye, you are somewhere new. You can go directly from A to Z and bypass all the letters in between. It does not really make sense how it happens, but *that* is a suddenly of God.

With God all things are possible. There is nothing He cannot do, nothing He cannot heal and nothing He cannot restore. No matter what you have suffered, regardless of how severe, it is possible to overcome because God is in the business of healing and restoration.

The definition of restoration: the act or process of returning something to its original condition.

When God restores us, He brings us back to our original condition: the purity and innocence of who we truly were before being damaged, hurt, abused or mistreated. It is not too late for you. No matter what you have been through, how old you are or what you have lost, God can and will restore you just as He did with Job. God restored not only what had been stolen from Job, but He went above and beyond so that Job prospered and his latter days were better than his former (see Job 42:12). Our God can restore time and years that were stolen (see Joel 2:25). He will take every crooked path in our lives and make it straight (see Isaiah 42:16). We will receive beauty in exchange for ashes, joy for mourning and praise in our hearts where there has been nothing but heaviness (see Isaiah 61:3).

It takes courage to stay the course. This Christian walk is not for the faint of heart. The secular world's misconception of Christians is so backward—that we are weak and use religion as a crutch because we are not strong enough to walk through life on our own. Ha! What a joke. The truth is, we are strong enough to realize we cannot walk through life successfully without God. Those of us who walk this walk know the level of strength required to go through the fire and keep going. We understand the absolute resolve demanded to hold onto our faith when all else fails. It is the narrow path to trust in God when nothing we see or feel makes sense, and few are willing to walk it. Only those with a steadfast heart and attitude are able to stay the course and finish this race.

> Do you not know that those who run in a race all run, but one receives the prize? Run in such a way that you may obtain it.
>
> 1 Corinthians 9:24

Our walk with God is not a sprint. It is an endurance run—a marathon! A marathon is 26.2 miles—as if 26 miles were not enough. Who the heck added on that .2? After 26 miles you are exhausted both physically and mentally, but I would bet that very few runners quit at the .2 mark. I do not care how fatigued you are, no one wants to give up after having already completed 26 miles with the finish line so close. In order to receive the prize, we must keep focused until the end and get across that line.

> Keep climbing. If you can't fly, run. If you can't run, walk. If you can't walk, crawl. But by all means, keep moving.
>
> Martin Luther King Jr.

I do not know about you, but even if I have to crawl over that line, I am finishing! God did not bring me this far to leave me here. I will finish, and I will receive the prize. In our race, we cannot always see the finish line, but it is closer than we might think. Many of us have been running for a long time and right now we have reached the 26-mile marker with only .2 to go. We are almost at the finish line, but we just don't know it! Sometimes, when it seems like we are the farthest away from victory, we are actually at the point right before our breakthrough. We may not realize it, but the very next step is across the finish line and into our Promised Land.

In the Bible, Joseph was given a promise from God that he would rule and reign. Then everything in his life went contrary for years. The final indignity came when he was wrongly accused by his master's wife and thrown into prison. In the natural realm it would seem as if he was farther from his destiny than ever, but really, he had reached the .2 mark. It may have appeared that Joseph was at his lowest low, but his very next step was being catapulted to the position right below the king, second in command in all the land. He went from prison directly into his promise. It makes no sense, but that is how God works. Our Lord is not linear. There is rarely a straight line to the promise. That is why it is impossible to accurately assess where we are by looking at our circumstances. We must have a spiritual perspective and remain in faith, because we are probably a lot closer than we think.

> Most people give up just when they're about to achieve success. They quit on the one-yard line. They give up at the last minute of the game one foot from a winning touchdown.
>
> Ross Perot

Waiting can be tiring, but we cannot give up! If we hold fast and stay in the game, the Lord will give us the strength we need to endure and finish.

> But those who wait on the LORD shall renew their strength; they shall mount up with wings like eagles, they shall run and not be weary, they shall walk and not faint.
>
> Isaiah 40:31

Mounting up with wings like eagles sounds good. That is what we all want, but perhaps you are not familiar with the extreme tribulation an eagle endures in the process of becoming the mighty and majestic bird that God created it to be.

It has been said that at least once in their lifetime all eagles undergo the molting process. They encounter a wilderness season that can bring with it a great depression. They lose their feathers, and their beaks and claws begin to alter as well. During this time they have no strength to fly, so they walk, like a turkey. They lose their ability to see as well. (Just as we can lose sight of where we are and where we are going when we are in our wilderness season.) When calcium builds up on the eagles' beaks, they can no longer hold up their heads. This is so traumatizing for the proud birds that they lose their desire to eat and have no strength to hunt for food. When the molting eagles move into this final state they will often begin to peck at one another, at times even killing another molting eagle as they gather together in one place. (Some of us have had an experience like this at church, of being judged and pecked at when we are going through our most difficult times.) At this stage the eagle will choose an area on a mountain range where the sun can shine directly on them, and they will lie on a rock and bathe in the sun. (The birds know that bathing in the sun, or like us, the Son, is the way to refresh when they are at their lowest point. Perhaps this is their own version of on-the-floor time!)

Some have observed other eagles dropping food to the ones going through this molting stage. Suddenly a sound splits the sky. A group of eagles flies overhead, screeching loudly, and drops fresh meat to the dying birds. It is believed that the screaming is encouragement from the soaring eagles to the molting ones. It is never the younger eagles that drop the food, but always the older eagles, the ones that have already survived this experience and know what the molting birds are going through. At this point the molting eagles have a choice: to accept the help and fight or to give up. They have been given what they need to go on, and some will do just that; they will rise up and take their rightful position in the sky. But some, unfortunately, will give up, choosing to remain there and die.

This is who I am to you now: I am your screaming eagle. I understand what you are going through. I have gone before you. I have been there, and I survived. I made it through, and you will, too.

God is no respecter of persons. What He did for me, He will do for you, too—as long as you keep going. You have what you need to fly. It is your time. Rise up and take your rightful position. If you do, in the end, you will stand before the Lord and be able to say, "I have fought the fight. I have finished the race. I have kept the faith."

You can do it! Don't give up!

Robia Scott began her professional career at the age of sixteen as a dancer and actress in Hollywood. After twenty years in the industry, Robia walked away from a thriving career in order to pursue her true calling in ministry. Her God-given gift of expression and communication of truth as an artist is now being fully utilized for the Kingdom of God.

Robia combines her knowledge and love of Scripture with a dynamic teaching style that is also down to earth and fun. She makes the deep things of God palatable by adhering to the wise words of Mary Poppins: "A spoonful of sugar helps the medicine go down!" Her ministry specializes in helping believers find wholeness and freedom by showing them how to appropriate all of what God promises in His Word in their lives. She is passionate that all Christians walk in their unique purpose and in the fullness of who God created them to be. Her heartfelt love for people and truth has her regularly traveling the country as a keynote speaker.

When at home, Robia can be found playing tennis, sipping cappuccinos and ministering alongside her husband, James. Together they are the founders and senior leaders of Deeper Life Church in Redondo Beach, California. Robia and James live in Orange County with their daughter, Gemma.

For more information on Robia Scott and Robia Ministries:
www.robiaministries.org
Facebook.com/RobiaScott
Twitter: @RobiaMinistries
Instagram: @RobiaScott